Monetary and Capital Markets Department

The Promise of Fintech: Financial Inclusion in the Post COVID-19 Era

Ratna Sahay, Ulric Eriksson von Allmen, Amina Lahreche, Purva Khera, Sumiko Ogawa, Majid Bazarbash, and Kim Beaton

INTERNATIONAL MONETARY FUND

Cataloging-in-Publication Data
IMF Library

Names: Sahay, Ratna. | Allmen, Ulric Eriksson von. | Lahrèche-Révil, Amina. | Khera, Purva. | Ogawa, Sumiko (Economist). | Bazarbash, Majid. | Beaton, Kim. | International Monetary Fund. Monetary and Capital Markets Department, issuing body. | International Monetary Fund, publisher.
Title: The promise of fintech : financial inclusion in the post COVID-19 era / Ratna Sahay, Ulric Eriksson von Allmen, Amina Lahreche, Purva Khera, Sumiko Ogawa, Majid Bazarbash, and Kim Beaton.
Other titles: Financial inclusion in the post COVID-19 era. | International Monetary Fund. Monetary and Capital Markets Department (Series).
Description: Washington, DC : International Monetary Fund, 2020. | At head of title: Monetary and Capital Markets Department. | Departmental paper series. | Includes bibliographical references.
Identifiers: ISBN 9781513512242 (paper)
Subjects: LCSH: Financial services industry—Technological innovations. | Financial services industry—Social aspects. | COVID-19 (Disease).
Classification: LCC HG173.S24 2020

The Departmental Paper Series presents research by IMF staff on issues of broad regional or cross-country interest. The views expressed in this paper are those of the author(s) and do not necessarily represent the views of the IMF, its Executive Board, or IMF management.

Publication orders may be placed online, by fax, or through the mail:
International Monetary Fund, Publication Services
P.O. Box 92780, Washington, DC 20090, U.S.A.
Tel. (202) 623-7430 Fax: (202) 623-7201
E-mail: publications@imf.org
www.imfbookstore.org
www.elibrary.imf.org

Contents

Acknowledgments

The authors are very grateful to many stakeholders across the IMF's membership—policy makers, central banks, regulatory bodies, banks, think tanks, fintech associations, and fintech companies—for providing invaluable insights during the interviews they conducted. The authors want to thank members of the IMF's Executive Board for facilitating many of the interviews, as well as Tobias Adrian, Jihad Alwazir, Bas Bakker, Nicolas Blancher, John Caparusso, Hector Carcel Villanova, Esha Chhabra, Jennifer Elliott, Yingjie Fan, Andrew Giddings, Simon Gray, Dirk Jan Grolleman, Abdullah Haron, Thor Jonasson, Nigel Jenkinson, Emanuel Kopp, Peter Kunzel, Frederik Lambert, Mindaugas Leika, Elena Loukoianova, Inutu Lukonga, Calvin McDonald, Tommaso Mancini Griffoli, Christopher Wilson, Maria Soledad Martinez Peria, Emmanuel Mathias, Hunter Monroe, Marina Moretti, Yen Mooi, Jennifer Moyo, William Murray, Jan Nolte, Kristel Poh, Umang Rawat, Scott Roger, Christoph Rosenberg, Mika Saito, Ghiath Shabsigh, Mauricio Soto, Olga Stankova, Tao Sun, Priscilla Toffano, Tomohiro Tsuruga, Patrizia Tumbarello, Nico Valckx, Fabian Valencia, and Bo Zhao, for comments that helped substantially improve the draft. Comments from Alfonso Garcia Mora (World Bank) are gratefully acknowledged. The authors are grateful to Cambridge Centre for Alternative Finance (CCAF) for gracefully sharing the cross country data on crowdfunding activity that were used to analyze marketplace lending. Finally, the authoring team gratefully acknowledges the excellent research assistance provided by Stephanie Ng and Elizabeth Mahoney, and wishes to thank Vanessa Guerrero and Angelica Marcela Mendez Acosta for their excellent administrative support throughout the project.

Glossary and Definitions

Glossary

AFI	Alliance for Financial Inclusion
ATM	automated teller machine
CCAF	Cambridge Centre for Alternative Finance
EMDE	emerging market and developing economy
FAS	Financial Access Survey
FATF	Financial Action Task Force
FDI	foreign direct investment
FIAP	Financial Inclusion Action Plan
FSB	Financial Stability Board
G7	Group of Seven
G20	Group of Twenty
G2P	government to person
GDP	gross domestic product
GPFI	Global Partnership for Financial Inclusion
GSMA	Global System for Mobile Communications Association

HP	Hodrick-Prescott Filter
IMF	International Monetary Fund
IT	information technology
ITU	International Telecommunication Union
MENA	Middle East and North Africa
ML/TF	money laundering/terrorism finance
NPCI	National Payment Corporation of India
NPL	nonperforming loan
OLS	ordinary least square
PCA	principal component analysis
PPP	purchasing power parity
P2P	peer-to-peer
SARS	severe acute respiratory syndrome
SDG	Sustainable Development Goal
SME	small- and medium-sized enterprise
UN	United Nations
UNSGSA	United Nations Secretary-General's Special Advocate
VC	venture capital
WB	World Bank

Definitions

Fintech	The technology-enabled innovation in financial services that could result in new business models, applications, processes, or products with an associated material effect on the provision of financial services.
Financial inclusion	Financial inclusion is defined as the "access to and use of formal financial services." It captures a range of financial services (notably transactions, savings, credit, and insurance) for individuals and firms (Sahay and others 2015b).
Digital financial inclusion or fintech-enabled financial inclusion	We use the two terms interchangeably in the paper. Digital access to and usage of formal financial services, such as through mobile phone (both smart and non-smart phones) and computers (to access the internet). This concept includes services provided by fintech companies and financial institutions.
Digital payment	Payment which is executed digitally. Includes payments using mobile phones or operated online. This does not include card payments.
Digital lending/credit	Credit activity that involves the extension of funds through digital means—via mobile phone or online. Digital lending can be extended through marketplace lending, peer-to-peer lending, e-commerce lending, online lending by banks, and mobile lending. Digital credit models typically make extensive used of digital data collection.
Marketplace lending	Lending via digital platforms which directly connects lenders to borrowers.
Mobile banking	Use of an application on a mobile device to access and execute banking services.
Mobile money	Financial service offered to its clients by a mobile network operator (or an entity partnering with a mobile network operator), which allows to transact and store value on a mobile phone. Mobile money is either facilitated by networks of mobile money agents, which operate the cash-in cash-out transactions or is linked to a bank account.

Executive Summary

Technology is changing the landscape of the financial sector, increasing access to financial services in profound ways. These changes have been in motion for several years, affecting nearly all countries in the world. During the COVID-19 pandemic, technology has created new opportunities for digital financial services to accelerate and enhance financial inclusion, amid social distancing and containment measures. At the same time, the risks emerging prior to COVID-19, as digital financial services developed, are becoming even more relevant.

Introducing a new index of digital financial inclusion, this paper shows that digital finance is increasing financial inclusion and is associated with higher GDP growth. These findings suggest that digital financial inclusion could play an important role in mitigating the economic and social impact of the ongoing COVID-19 crisis. Broadening the financial access of low-income households and small businesses could also support a more inclusive recovery. These potentials, however, cannot be taken for granted, as the pandemic could accelerate pre-existing risks of financial exclusion, and give rise to new risks to the fintech sector itself.

Digital financial services are faster, more efficient, and typically cheaper than traditional financial services and, therefore, increasingly reaching lower-income households and small- and medium-sized enterprises (SMEs). During the COVID-19 health crisis, digital financial services can and are enabling contactless and cashless transactions. Where digital financial inclusion is advanced, they are helping facilitate the efficient and quick deployment of government support measures, including to people and firms affected by the pandemic.

Our quantitative analysis is supplemented by interviews with stakeholders, including representatives of more than 70 fintech companies, central banks, regulatory bodies, and banks. These interviews helped to gain insights on the potential of fintech for financial inclusion, the competitive landscape, the impediments, the role of regulation, and the risks.

Digital finance is increasing financial inclusion, complementing or substituting traditional finance. While digital financial services are still small relative to traditional services, they are growing rapidly and at varying speed across regions and countries. In all the 52 countries covered in our analysis, digital financial inclusion increased between 2014 and 2017, even where traditional financial inclusion was stalling or declining. Digital financial inclusion is evolving from "spend" to "lend," and tends to fill a gap: both payments and lending develop where the traditional delivery of financial services is less present.

Notwithstanding the early stages of digital finance, our empirical analysis already points to its positive association with GDP growth, using an approach that addresses potential reverse causality. Going forward, this is an important finding for creating income and employment, and for reducing inequalities in financial access following the large COVID-19 shock.

Fintech appears to be closing gender gaps, but special attention would need to be paid to ensure that women are not left behind during the COVID-19 crisis. Stakeholders noted several barriers to digital financial inclusion such as access to resources (mobile phone, internet), cultural or social norms, and digital and financial literacy, may be higher for women.

Our data analysis as well as interviews confirm that the delivery of digital financial services is evolving with various models of interaction between incumbents and disruptors. Fintech companies—which are frequently at the source of the innovation—often compete with banks and other established financial institutions, with the latter responding by investing heavily in fintech. But we also see widespread collaboration based on complementarities. Both trends are likely to accelerate post-COVID as fintech companies and financial institutions seize new opportunities.

This crisis is the first test of resilience of fintech companies, and the competitive landscape could change permanently during the recovery. The tightening of funding conditions and a sharp drop in transactions due to weak demand is already hitting fintech companies hard, especially the smaller ones and those with thinner buffers. Widespread consolidation in the fintech industry and retrenchment by smaller companies could lead to greater concentration in the sector and reduce financial access of small customers.

Financial inclusion itself could be at risk, driven by unequal access to digital infrastructure and potential biases amplified by new data sources and data analytics. Lack of access to mobile phones, computers, or the internet could lead to new forms of exclusion, which could be exacerbated as the shift to digital financial services accelerates during and post COVID-19.

During the COVID-19 crisis, access to government electronic systems that are well integrated with digital financial services platforms such as fintech firms, mobile money companies, and digital banking are proving to be critical in providing wide-reaching policy support promptly and without physical contact. If they are not easily accessible or not well integrated, fiscal support announcements—no matter how large—will fail to reach those most vulnerable and needy. Thus, the fiscal response should go hand-in-hand with investment in digital infrastructure, and importantly promoting digital and financial literacy to ensure greater digital inclusion.

Accelerating growth of digital financial services could also present financial stability risks if their regulation and supervision does not keep pace. In our discussions, regulators also warned that cybersecurity risks or inappropriate lending practices by underregulated institutions could jeopardize trust. Policymakers will also need to consider novel approaches to ensure high-quality supervision and regulation, support the safe use of innovative technologies, while ensuring that regulation remain proportionate to the risks. Fortunately, supervisors across countries have recognized the need to adapt regulatory approaches that strike the right balance between enabling financial innovation and address challenges and risks to financial integrity, consumer protection, and financial stability. In addition, policymakers should aspire for international agreements on data privacy, cybersecurity, digital identification, cross-border digital currencies, and regulation of Big Techs to ensure that the fintech landscape remains sufficiently competitive in the post-COVID era.

Chapter

1 Introduction

Somewhere remote in a low-income country, in the early hours of the morning, a woman wakes up and dials her cell phone. She is borrowing a very small amount of money digitally to buy vegetables in the local market. During the day, she will sell her inventory in her shop located in the outskirts of the town. Some customers will pay her using their mobile wallet, others with cash. She will transfer the cash onto her phone at the shop next door, where the merchant is also a mobile money agent. At the end of the day, she will be able to pay back her loan and keep her profit in her mobile wallet. She can use this mobile money to pay for the gas she uses to cook dinner, as the utility company has recently connected its payment system to the mobile money infrastructure. In her daily life, this is huge progress.

Somewhere central in a rich country, just a few weeks before the winter holiday season, a machine in a chocolate factory breaks down. Without a new device, the profits during the busiest part of the year will vanish. The owner tries frantically to obtain credit from his bank to replace his machine. Even though the factory has operated for several years and has a profitable track record, the bank is just too busy for this small client and schedules an appointment in the new year—way too late. A few years ago, this could have been the end of the business. But a friend told him about an online lender. Within a week, the online lender had assessed the creditworthiness, approved the loan, and disbursed the money. The machine was delivered just in time—two weeks before Christmas. This is a true story that played out in the city of London.

These anecdotes that preceded the COVID-19 pandemic illustrate ways in which fintech has enhanced financial inclusion in countries at different stages of development. Globally 1.7 billion people have no access to a bank account and small- and medium-sized enterprises (SMEs) (95 percent of companies worldwide) provide employment to more than 60 percent of workers, yet struggle to access finance. In this environment, fintech (technological innovation in the financial sector) is creating significant opportunities, helped by the growing ownership of mobile phones and access to internet.

The COVID-19 health crisis has created new opportunities for digital financial services to accelerate financial inclusion amid social distancing.[1] The health crisis led to the "Great Lockdown," as country authorities have opted for restrictive containment measures—lockdowns, quarantines, travel restrictions, and other social distancing measures—to bring the contagion of the virus under control. Fintech, including mobile money, can help people and firms to maintain and increase access to financial services during lockdowns and the reopening of businesses, given growing preference for cashless and contactless transactions to mitigate the spread. Many country authorities have encouraged its use by introducing measures to lower cost and increasing the limits on transactions for digital transactions (e.g., Ghana, Kenya, Myanmar, among others). These developments could help accelerate the shift toward digital financial services from traditional financial services. For instance, the severe acute respiratory syndrome (SARS) epidemic in 2003 accelerated China's launching of digital payments and e-commerce (World Economic Forum).[2]

Anecdotal evidence suggests that fintech is already playing an important role in mitigating the economic impact of the COVID-19, by facilitating targeted fiscal measures to be deployed efficiently and quickly to their intended beneficiaries, even the unbanked. By reducing or eliminating the need for physical interactions and the need for cash, fintech is helping governments reach—quickly and securely—people and businesses with various forms of income and liquidity support. In countries where access to banking networks is limited, mobile money networks are being used to deliver government transfers (e.g., Namibia, Peru, Uganda, Zambia). Information from data garnered from mobile payments is connecting governments to informal workers outside formal benefits programs. In Togo, for example, a new program was introduced targeting informal workers, in which transfers are made through mobile money and with a top-up for women recipients (IMF 2020). Tax authorities are encouraging use of online platforms for filing tax returns (Kenya, Namibia, and Nigeria). Some fintech lenders are also responding quickly to the liquidity needs of SMEs affected by the pandemic (e.g., China), taking advantage of the real-time data and online processes. Many fintech companies, big and small, are offering flexibility in loan repayments for impacted borrowers (e.g., India, Kenya, and United Kingdom). But the

[1]Agur, Martinez Peria, and Celine Rochon (2020) analyze the opportunities and risks associated with digital financial services in the context of the COVID-19 pandemic.

[2]https://www.weforum.org/agenda/2020/05/digital-payments-cash-and-COVID-19-pandemics/

scope to improve remains vast, especially in expanding e-government via fintech companies and digital banking.

From a macroeconomic perspective and based on recent empirical evidence, the promise of digital financial inclusion in enhancing economic growth, narrowing income inequalities, and reducing poverty appears to be immense.[3] From poor households to SMEs, fintech has been facilitating access to accounts, transactions, and credit in recent years, thereby opening opportunities for wider sections of the population to participate in formal economic activity. The development of digital savings, cross-border transfer solutions, and insurance also offers promises. Beyond the enhancement of individual opportunities, a broader access to finance has positive macroeconomic effects: IMF research already shows that financial inclusion supports growth and lowers inequality (Sahay and others 2015a, and Čihák and Sahay 2020) and, provided the financial sector is well regulated, it does not hurt financial stability. It also improves the effectiveness of macroeconomic policies, further supporting growth and stability (Loukoianova and Yang 2018). These are important finding for creating income and employment, and for reducing inequalities in financial access following the large COVID-19 shock.

Notwithstanding these opportunities, the COVID-19 crisis has also brought to the fore risks that had been emerging prior to the pandemic. For instance, risks to financial stability—notably as regulatory arbitrage leads financial activities to migrate from the regulated to the less or lightly regulated sector—are one important concern of policymakers. The possible disruption of traditional business models, and the interconnectedness of traditional financial institutions with lightly supervised fintech companies raise similar concerns. There are also risks related to the technology itself, which affect both banks and nonbank financial institutions: for instance, confidential data may leak, including via cyberattacks. Financial service providers could be facing new money laundering/terrorism finance (ML/TF) risks. Regulators warned that cybersecurity risks or inappropriate lending practices by under-regulated institutions could jeopardize trust. The balance of risks may also be affected by the possible changes in the fintech landscape and regulations during and post COVID-19.

Financial inclusion itself could be at risk as digital services accelerate in the post-COVID era, driven by unequal access to digital infrastructure and potential biases amplified by new data sources and data analytics. Lack of access to mobile phones, computers, or the internet could leave us with new forms of exclusion, which could be exacerbated if the shift toward digi-

[3]Financial inclusion enabled by the use of fintech. In this note, the words "digital" and "fintech-driven" financial inclusion are used interchangeably, although the former could be offered by financial institutions as well (see Box 1).

tal financial services accelerates during and post COVID-19. During the COVID-19 crisis, smooth access to government electronic systems that are well integrated with digital financial services platforms such as fintech firms, mobile money companies, and digital banking are proving to be critical in providing wide-reaching policy support promptly and without contact to the public. If they are not easily accessible or not well integrated, fiscal support announcements—no matter how large—will fail to reach the most vulnerable and needy. Fintech companies also highlighted the limited supply of skilled labor and digital infrastructure as major constraints. Data biases or inaccurate and insufficient information could result in greater financial exclusion and feed distrust for new technology, especially amongst the most vulnerable. Lack of financial and digital literacy could exacerbate these risks. Financial inclusion could be threatened from the possible demise of microfinance institutions, whose operations and clients might be affected more by the economic fallout and who might be struggling to operate digitally during the COVID-19 crisis.

Furthermore, many fintech companies are young and have never experienced an economic downturn before, let alone faced the worst global shock in several decades. The COVID-19 crisis is the first major test of the fintech sector's resilience during a crisis. First, tighter funding conditions will affect fintech companies, big or small, with thinner liquidity buffers. Preliminary data already suggest this is happening: fintech funding activity stalled in the first quarter of 2020, resulting in the worst first quarter for fintech funding since 2017, as investors pulled back investments.[4] In so far as the funding draught leads to smaller fintech firms being bought up by larger firms, or disappearing altogether, we could see higher market concentration in the fintech sector going forward. Second, the economic crisis, and in particular the collapse in consumption (notably in highly impacted sectors such as hotels, restaurant, airlines, and even retail) will cause a fall in fintech payments firms' revenues.[5] Third, much fintech lending has targeted small borrowers, who are likely to be disproportionately affected in the ongoing crisis, and hence may see a sharp deterioration in loan quality. Major disruptions to services provided by fintech companies could set back the progress that has been made with digital financial inclusion and innovation, and there could also be macroeconomic and financial spillovers.

While fintech's potential to increase financial inclusion is clearly very high, the benefits and risks cannot be easily quantified. The data on digital payments are patchy, even patchier for digital lending, savings, and insurance (the other three components of financial inclusion). Financial inclusion, a key

[4]https://www.cbinsights.com/research/report/fintech-trends-q1-2020/

[5]Some payments companies have seen demand for their services take off. For instance, PayPal job slots have more than doubled so far this year, according to the Thinknum job posting database.

component of United Nations Sustainable Development Goal (SDG), would remain elusive if policymakers cannot accurately measure the benefits and risks. Hence, a concerted effort is needed to strengthen data collection, and this would be an important early step in the COVID-19 economic recovery phase, once the immediate health risk fades.

Recognizing the data limitations, this paper uses a two-pronged approach to further our understanding of developments in digital financial inclusion and their macroeconomic effects. It complements quantitative analysis, based on available data from before the COVID-19 crisis, with information from interviews around the world with a broad set of policymakers, regulators, fintech companies, and banks. In a fast-evolving fintech landscape, the interviews allowed us to understand better developments—both prior to and post the COVID-19 pandemic—that are not yet captured in the data.

Our work focuses on two leading aspects of financial inclusion: access to domestic payments and credit. The other dimensions of financial inclusion—saving, insurance, and wealth management—are still nascent, and where they exist, data are lacking. The potential for fintech to support affordable cross-border payments—notably for remittances—is high; the cost of remitting money across border is declining slowly, but at almost 7 percent, it remains above the 3 percent target set by the SDGs. Fintech combined with strong digital identification and robust ML/FT could have a great potential in supporting more affordable and remotely accessible cross-border transaction such as remittances that have been an important support for families in low-income countries. The latter topic, however, is beyond the scope of this note, which focuses on domestic payments and credit.

We introduce a new index to measure digital financial inclusion. Comparing this index with one of traditional financial inclusion allows us to quantify the relative progress of digital financial inclusion in a sample of 52 emerging market and developing economies (EMDEs) prior to the COVID-19 crisis. We also analyze global developments in marketplace lending, one aspect of digital credit. Finally, we explore the determinants of digital financial inclusion, and assess its impact on economic growth.

To complement the empirical analysis, we interviewed representatives of more than 70 fintech companies, central banks, regulatory bodies, and banks around the world in two phases (Annex 1). The first phase of interviews were conducted before the COVID-19 crisis, and they provided key insights on the areas where fintech has the greatest potential for financial inclusion, the competitive landscape, the impediments to promoting digital financial inclusion, the role of regulation, and the risks related to digital financial inclusion. The second phase involved follow-up interviews with a subsample of the fintech companies interviewed in the first phase to understand the impact of the

COVID-19 pandemic on digital financial inclusion; their own business and clients; their responses and collaboration with governments and traditional banks; and on how they see their roles going forward.

Our key findings underscore the impact of digital finance and the factors that may facilitate or inhibit financial inclusion. In particular,

- *Digital finance is increasing financial inclusion, even where traditional financial inclusion is declining.* In all the 52 countries covered in our analysis, digital financial inclusion improved between 2014 and 2017, particularly in Africa and Asia, and even where traditional financial inclusion was stalling or declining. In a sample of more than 100 countries, marketplace lending—a subset of digital credit—also grew fast, albeit from a small base. Digital financial inclusion tends to fill a gap: it develops where the traditional delivery of financial services is less present. Interviews point to different effects on digital credit during the COVID-19 crisis—in some countries fintech lenders participate in the government schemes to support credit extension to SMEs, whereas in other countries many fintech forms are scaling down new lending in response to weak demand and to focus on preserving liquidity and managing credit risks.
- *Digital financial inclusion is associated with higher GDP growth.* We find that adoption of digital payments is significantly and positively associated with growth, consistent with the notion that fintech might contribute to growth. Fintech could thus play an important role in mitigating the economic impact of the COVID-19 pandemic, and support the recovery, as countries with higher digital financial inclusion will find it relatively easier to (1) ensure continued access to financial services, including by maintaining credit flows to households and businesses while keeping people safe; (2) deliver government support effectively and securely; and (3) support consumption, innovation, and hence productivity through digital economy developments. However, the impact on growth and income distribution in the post-COVID era may also be affected by the possible changes in the fintech landscape—if the smaller fintech companies which have higher reach to low-income households and small businesses disappear, it may increase the income divide between the rich and poor.
- *Fintech is contributing toward closing gender gaps in financial inclusion in most countries, but there is a concern that they may rise in the post-COVID era.* Stakeholders noted several barriers that may be higher for women: cultural or social norms, financial literacy, safety, and disparity in access to resources. Given these structural barriers, concerns remain that the gender gaps may widen as the shift toward digital financial services accelerates during the COVID-19 crisis.
- *The delivery of digital financial services is evolving, with various models of interaction between incumbents and disruptors.* Fintech companies—

frequently the source of the innovation—often compete with banks and other established financial institutions. These established institutions are responding to the competition by investing heavily in fintech. But we also see widespread collaboration between fintech firms and established institutions, based on complementarities. This was confirmed by our data analysis as well as interviews. While the COVID-19 could increase both the opportunities for collaboration and competition as traditional institutions accelerate the shift toward digitization, policy measures focused on delivering support related to the COVID-19 through the banking sector could affect the competitive landscape. Consolidation in the fintech industry, driven for example, by tighter funding conditions for smaller fintech firms, could lead to greater concentration in the sector. At the same time, the COVID-19 crisis is also illustrating the opportunities for governments to collaborate more with private digital financial service providers to increase the reach of e-government services to wider sections of the population.

- *The safe development of digital financial inclusion rests on a combination of factors.* Rapid financial inclusion without proper regulation and financial literacy can lead to financial instability, as witnessed during the global financial crisis. Regulators warned that cybersecurity risks or inappropriate lending practices by underregulated institutions could jeopardize trust—in this context, consumer protection, digital identification, and financial/digital literacy were high on their agenda. Fintech companies highlighted the supply of skilled labor for fintech companies and availability of digital financial infrastructure as major constraints.
- *Digital finance can create new risks to financial inclusion.* Those risks stem from unequal access to digital infrastructure, constraints to financial and digital literacy, and potential biases amplified by new data sources and data analytics. The current model of lightly regulated digital lending could, in turn, threaten financial stability. Indirect risks relate to the possible disruption of financial inclusion through microfinance institutions, and to the consequences of a demise in trust in digital technology. All of these risks are even more important in light of the rapid and abrupt shift toward digital financial services amidst the COVID-19 crisis, as highlighted above.

Analyses on digital financial inclusion face constraints, many of which originate from lack of comprehensive data on certain aspects of fintech-related financial inclusion. First, the data do not fully capture all financial services, such as savings/wealth management and insurance instruments and many aspects related to credit. They also exclude cross-border payments services (Figure 1). Second, detailed data on digital payments is available only for a relatively small sample of countries (52 out of about 190) and excludes the period from the onset of the COVID-19 health crisis as well as advanced economies. Third, the databases we use to capture digital services do not identify the provider—in other words, such data could reflect services pro-

Figure 1. Scope of the Analysis

Of the many dimensions of financial services that are affected by fintech innovations, our work focuses on payments and credit.

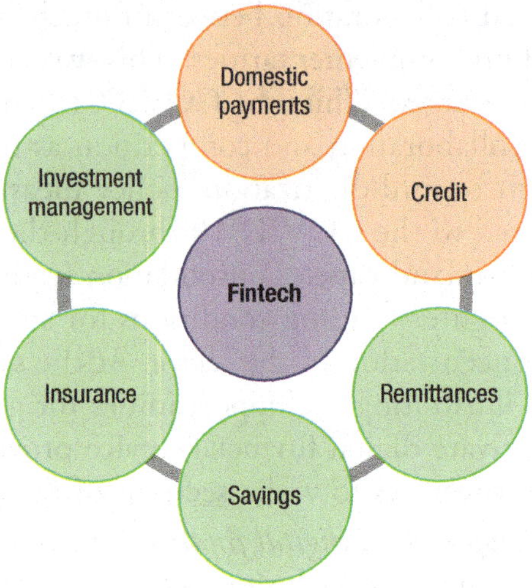

Source: IMF staff.

vided by fintech companies, as well as banks. Fourth, in the empirical analysis on the impact of digital finance on growth, the available time series is short and excludes several components of digital finance and, therefore, likely underestimates the impact on growth. Fifth, determining the direction of causality between growth and fintech-related financial inclusion remains a challenge, not unique to the empirical work in this paper. Even though our analysis attempts to address endogeneity or reverse causality, the short time span of the data and lack of good instruments remain constraints. Finally, even though we interviewed many stakeholders around the globe, the sample may not be sufficiently representative of the population.

The remainder of the paper is organized around six broad questions that were covered in the interviews and the empirical work. A short review of the literature sets the stage for those questions. Then, the paper asks the following: Where was digital financial inclusion emerging prior to the COVID-19 crisis? Is fintech increasing financial inclusion? What are the macroeconomic effects of digital financial inclusion? Are fintech companies disrupting traditional providers, and how could these relationships evolve during the ongoing downturn and the subsequent recovery? What are the impediments to the development of digital financial inclusion? What are the risks of fintech to financial inclusion? The last section offers some open questions on the changing landscape of the fintech sector from the COVID-19 and its implications for financial inclusion.

Chapter

2 Setting the Stage: Recent Global Developments and Literature Review

Three fundamental changes have influenced the development of fintech: massive data generation, advances in computer algorithms, and increases in processing power. These have been facilitated by high-speed broadband internet, cloud computing, and artificial intelligence, which have enabled big data analytics, blockchain technology, and biometric identification.

Fintech is changing the way financial services are delivered to small businesses and low-income households. Traditionally, financial services have been delivered by banks and their agents, microfinance institutions, and informal systems (for instance relying on relatives, microlending clubs, or money lenders), with often limited competition. They are predominantly built on cash transactions and face-to-face interactions with the financial service provider. Those interactions are the basis for monitoring creditworthiness; they are also often the way customers become financially educated. The emergence of fintech is changing this landscape: with the development of digital finance tools that are accessible from mobile phones or computers, the need for face-to-face interactions is greatly reduced. The mobility restrictions to contain the current COVID-19 pandemic have amplified these benefits of expanding digital financial services. The development of digital platforms, which can offer a variety of financial products and serve as aggregators for existing financial products or fintech companies' own products, helps maximize the value for customer by facilitating a comparison of the price and suitability of products and services offered by different companies.

Fintech's potential to boost financial inclusion has been on the radar of global leaders and policymakers, since long before the COVID-19 crisis. The Alliance for Financial Inclusion (AFI), a global network of policymakers, started in 2008, and set out its main objectives in the Maya Declaration in 2011. The G20 leaders also focused on financial inclusion in the Seoul Summit in 2010, endorsing a Financial Inclusion Action Plan (FIAP) and creating the Global Partnership for Financial Inclusion (GPFI). In 2015, the United Nations adopted SDGs for 2030, wherein financial inclusion features prominently. In 2016, the AFI and GPFI identified technology as a core aspect of financial inclusion, creating a new workstream, Fintech for Financial Inclusion. In 2018, at their Annual Meetings in Indonesia, the IMF and World Bank launched the Bali Fintech Agenda, which lays out the broad principles for the safe development of fintech, including to support financial inclusion. The COVID-19 pandemic has put a bright spotlight on how digital financial inclusion can be harnessed to respond to the crisis and how the crisis in turn would accelerate digital financial inclusion.

The international attention has spurred data collection and analysis on financial inclusion on a cross-country basis. The early literature largely relied on survey work in individual countries, or on single measures of financial inclusion—such as the number of bank branches and ATM and bank accounts per capita (e.g., Beck and others 2007; Honohan 2008). The launch of databases such as the IMF's Financial Access Survey (FAS) and the World Bank's Global Findex database (Demirgüç-Kunt and Klapper 2012) allowed the development and use of more multidimensional, composite measures of financial inclusion, taking into account various aspects of access and usage by household and firms (Amidžić Massara, and Mialou 2014; Dabla-Norris and others 2015a; Camara and Tuesta 2017).[1] This, in turn, opened the way for analyzing the macroeconomic impact (Sahay and others 2015a; Sahay and others 2015b; Svirydzenka 2016, Dabla-Norris and others, 2015b; Loukoianova and Yang 2018) and drivers of financial inclusion (Deléchat and others 2018; Rojas-Suárez and Amado 2014; Rojas-Suárez 2016).

The empirical literature on *digital* financial inclusion is nascent and mostly focuses on specific countries or regions. It includes work on the development of mobile money in Kenya (Tarazi and Breloff 2010; Jack and Suri 2011, 2014; IMF 2018b), as well as analysis of regional developments in fintech activities (Sy and others 2019, focus on sub-Saharan Africa; Berkmen and others 2019, on Latin America and the Caribbean; Loukoianova and others 2019, on Pacific Islands; and Lukonga 2018, and Blancher and others, 2019, on Middle East and Central Asia). Heterogeneity in the adoption of mobile money across regions and countries are typically explained by GDP growth, levels of per capital income, the regulatory environment (Tarazi and Breloff 2010; Gutierrez and Singh 2013), and rule of law. The pivotal role of a lead firm, such as the Ant Financial Services Group in China, is also recognized (Hau and others 2018). Some studies analyze the impact of mobile money and the internet (Loukoianova and Yang 2018; Jahan and others

[1]There are two parametric approaches used for constructing these composite indices: principal component analysis (PCA) and common factor analysis.

2019) and the drivers of mobile money adoption (Lashitew van Tulder, and Liasse 2019).

Two recent interview-based studies of fintech providers and regulators have enriched our understanding of the role of fintech in financial inclusion. Patwardhan, Singleton, and Schmitz (2018) underscore the importance of mobile and other person-to-person payment methods, and the development of new ways of complying with customer due diligence. Citi (2020) similarly emphasize the role of identity, mobile money, platform-based services, and microcredit. Their findings are consistent with our findings.

However, to the best of our knowledge, there are no comprehensive global studies on fintech and financial inclusion, reflecting in part the limited availability of cross-country data. Some studies have looked into the role of fintech in supporting access to credit—an important dimension of financial inclusion which is often cited as a key constraint to activity, especially for SMEs (Ayyagari Demirgüç-Kunt, and Maksimovic 2017). An important part of the literature has focused on understanding the determinants of digital lending, underscoring the importance of regulation, financial development, digital infrastructure or market structure (Rau 2019; Claessens and others 2018). Studies using individual loan data suggest that fintech lenders process mortgage applications faster than traditional lenders (Fuster and others 2018), do reach underserved customers and offer lower-cost credit than traditional lenders (Jagtiani and Lemieux 2017; de Roure Pelizzon, and Thakor 2018).

Finally, the analysis of potential stability and inclusion risks related to fintech is still at an early stage, both in the fintech-related literature and at the level of global standard setters. As the financial sector continues to see disruptions—including from the entry of Big Tech (large technology firms with a dominant role in online activity)—the discussions are increasingly focused on privacy concerns, ML/TF risks, and the potential macroeconomic impact of digital currencies (Adrian and Mancini-Griffoli 2019; Brunnermeier, Harold, and Landau 2019; and G7 2019). The financial stability implications of the increasing interconnectedness between fintech companies and banks, or of the growing digital credit origination, are also on the agenda of regulators. Finally, awareness of the risk that fintech could lead to financial exclusion—e.g., because of lack of access to digital infrastructure, differences in financial and digital illiteracy, or potential biases in algorithms—is yet to gain traction. These risks might increase with the abrupt switch toward digital financial services amid the COVID-19 crisis, including for making government-to-person (G2P) payments.

Chapter

3 Where Is Fintech for Financial Inclusion Emerging?

Fintech-driven financial services are filling a gap left by traditional financial institutions. Across different regions in the world, fintech companies are making their presence felt locally. Some companies, including in Silicon Valley, the United Kingdom, and China, are also expanding into emerging markets, such as India, Kenya, Mexico, Nigeria, and Tanzania. Traditional financial institutions typically provide services through brick-and-mortar establishments and rely on legacy technology that are costly to operate, and even more costly to upgrade and adapt to fast-changing technology. But, as discussed later, these institutions are responding to the competition from fintech companies with large investments in technology. Fintech companies are often better positioned to use the latest technology and data analytics to target niche markets, including lower-income groups, and orient their products to maximize consumer satisfaction. During and after the COVID-19 health crisis, these characteristics can allow them to help governments expand the reach of their emergency responses to those in the informal sector and those who don't have access to bank accounts.

In most countries, fintech for financial inclusion started with "spend" and is fast moving into "lend." The growth of mobile money—one of the early fintech solutions for payments—has been most prevalent in EMDEs. Online digital *payments* are more common in advanced economies and some emerging markets. In both cases, digital payments generate data, which financial institutions can use to build creditworthiness assessments that do not require long histories, identity, or collateral. These developments in turn enable digital lending. The ability to track payment transaction records could also provide information on which sectors are suffering the largest consumption declines during the ongoing COVID-19 crisis, and, therefore allow for targeted credit provisioning, including government assistance to firms and households. Digital *lending* so far is concentrated in China, the United Kingdom and the United States, but is growing rapidly in other parts of the world, such as India and Kenya. Interviews with fintech companies indicate that they are eager to expand into lending to ensure viability, as profitability is low (or even negative) in the payments business.

Spend: What We Know About Digital Payments

Digital payments have so far been the most common instrument of financial inclusion and can be expected to accelerate during the post-COVID era. Successful mobile money services require a large enough network of users and an ability to link cash and mobile money transactions. In their simplest form, they use feature phones, allowing individuals and merchants to transact without physical cash. The progress to date is striking is some parts of the world. Stakeholders, especially in Africa, underscored the convenience factor as the most useful aspects of mobile money: the investment cost is low (basic mobile phones can be enough, and smart phones are not essential), it is simple to use, it is available any time of the day, and it avoids long and costly trips to the nearest town that has a bank or an ATM.[1,2] It is also safer in comparison to using cash, as it reduces the risk of theft. These benefits may seem rudimentary but are transformational for improving daily lives of the underprivileged. Moreover, the COVID-19 pandemic has magnified these benefits, and not just for the underprivileged: digital payments allow people and firms to conduct financial services while adhering to the social distancing recommended to reduce contagion.

Africa and Asia have seen the largest increase in digital payments, with East Africa, China, and India taking the lead. In Africa, fintech has taken the form of mobile money—impressively cutting the cost of sending remittances by 50 percent (GSMA 2016, using the World Bank's Remittance Prices Worldwide database). It originated in Kenya and is rapidly expanding to the rest of the continent. In China and India, online payments and messaging apps prompted the development of fintech services. In all cases, the development of digital money was spurred by systemic actors, such as M-Pesa in Kenya, Alipay and Wechat Pay in China, and Paytm in India. As Figure 2 indicates, mobile phone ownership is widespread among both men and women, even though it is less for the latter.

Empirical evidence points to the growing importance of mobile money payment services in low-income countries. Data from the World Bank and the GSMA points to the growing usage of digital payments, using either mobile phones or the internet.

[1]Smartphones are becoming increasingly affordable, with some costing US$20 to US$30.

[2]Even in advanced economies, digital payments reduce cash usage (see Fung, Huynh, and Sabetti 2014, on Canada).

Figure 2. Access to Mobile Phones, 2017

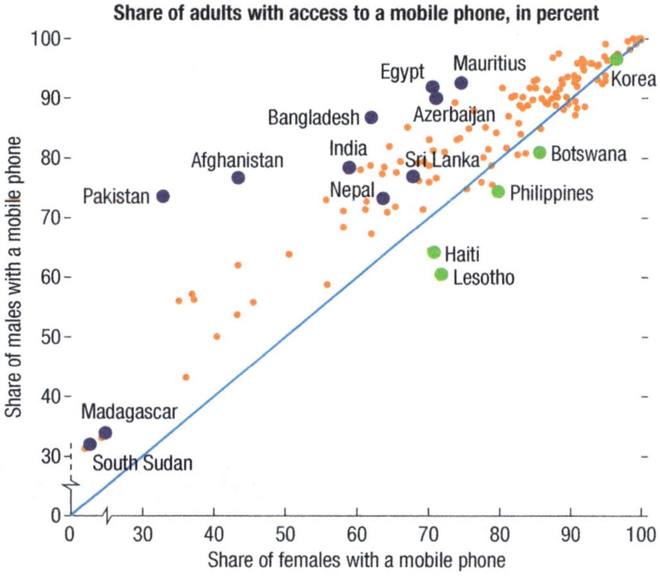

Source: World Bank, G20 Financial Inclusion Indicators.
Note: Green (purple) indicate examples of countries with higher female (male) ownership of mobile phones than male (female).

- The number of active mobile money accounts almost tripled and the use of mobile phone for domestic remittances roughly doubled between 2013 and 2017 in lower-middle and low-income countries (Figure 3). As a result, in low-income countries, about half of the population received or sent remittances using mobile phones in 2017. The value of mobile money transaction now constitutes a substantial part of the financial system, with transactions in Cambodia, Ghana, and Zimbabwe, reaching more than 75 percent of GDP in 2018 (Figure 4).
- A parallel development is observed in online payments (partly made on smartphones): the share of adults making or receiving digital payments increased by 11 percentage points between 2014 and 2017, to reach 52 percent (Demirgüç-Kunt and others 2018).
- In 2017, more than 2.9 million mobile money agents operating in 90 countries facilitated cash-in/cash-out transactions, peer-to-peer transfers, and bill payments (GSMA 2018).

The COVID-19 crisis and related government responses will further stoke growth in digital financial services. Measures introduced by many country authorities—lowering fees and increasing limits on mobile money transactions (e.g., Kenya, Uganda, and Zambia) or to ease know your customer (KYC) regulations for small transactions (e.g., Ghana) and to relax interop-

Figure 3. Mobile Money Accounts, 2013–17
(Active, per 1,000 adults)

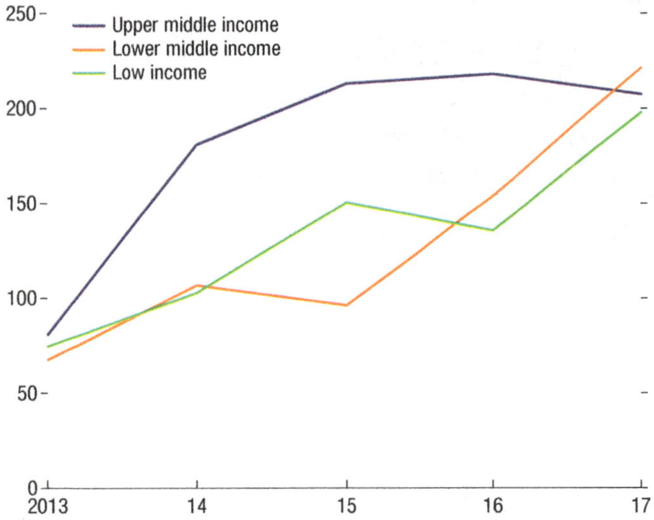

Sources: IMF Financial Access Survey; and IMF staff calculations.

Figure 4. Value of Mobile Money Transactions, 2018
(Percent of GDP)

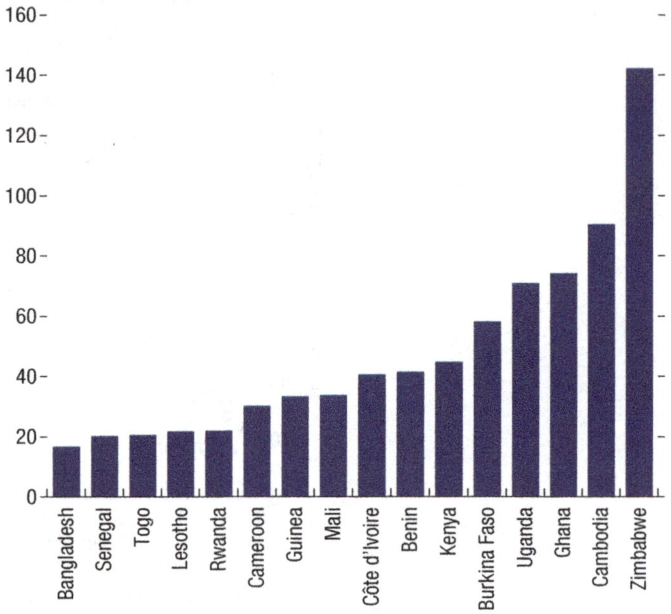

Source: IMF Financial Access Survey.

erability rules (Democratic Republic of Congo)—could accelerate the shift toward digital financial services, including by traditional financial institutions. Moreover, it could lead to an increase in the collaboration between governments and fintech service providers to expand the reach of governments' support measures. For example, Peruvian authorities are expanding the set of financial service providers to channel G2P—to include private banks and mobile money providers—to reach additional beneficiaries.

Lend: From Payment Data to Microcredit

The development of mobile money and online payments, and the expansion of user data that comes with it, has spurred digital lending. Ant Financial in China, a global leader in mobile and online financial services, started as a payments service and expanded into providing digital credit. Digital lenders use "alternative data" (from payments providers, and other sources such as the internet) and "loan engines" (e.g., innovative algorithms) to identify creditworthy clients and provide (mostly unsecured) lending. Fintech companies in the United States have grown to make up 38 percent of the unsecured personal loan market in 2018, from only 5 percent in 2013 (TransUnion 2019). In the United Kingdom, SMEs are an obvious target of fintech companies as they receive only 2 percent of bank loans, even though they contribute to 50 percent of GDP and 70 percent of employment.

The role of digital lenders during the COVID-19 crisis appears to vary across countries and by institution. With online platforms and real-time data, some established digital lenders are responding quickly to the liquidity needs of SMEs affected by COVID-19 related lockdowns and containment measures (e.g., in China and the United Kingdom). Their technology- and online-focused business models give them an advantage over traditional financial institutions in digital verification and onboarding of new customers, particularly so amid the need for social distancing. On the other hand, some fintech lenders noted having halted new lending during the COVID-19 lockdown, in response to weak demand and in order to preserve liquidity and focus on managing credit risks of their existing portfolio. Some are taking part in the governments' emergency lending programs, but the extent varies across countries, depending on whether these programs are designed exclusively for banks or are open to nonbank lenders more broadly (e.g., United Kingdom and United States).

Marketplace lending—one source of digital lending for which comparable cross-country data exists—remains small but doubled from 2015 to 2017. By 2017, it reached US$400 billion, largely driven by consumer credit (Figure 5). The volume of marketplace lending remains very small, however, at less than 0.5 percent of GDP for most countries. In 2017, Fintech credit was dominated by China, followed by the United States and the United Kingdom— together, they made up 98 percent of the fintech credit market.[3] There are differences across countries according to the type of lending, with consumer credit fairly dominant in Middle Eastern and Central Asian countries and the United States, and business lending dominating in the United Kingdom, non-US Western Hemisphere, and Asia (Figure 6).

[3]Marketplace lending is likely to have declined substantially in China after 2017, following regulatory changes.

Figure 5. Global Fintech Lending by Main Segments, 2015–17
(US$ billion)

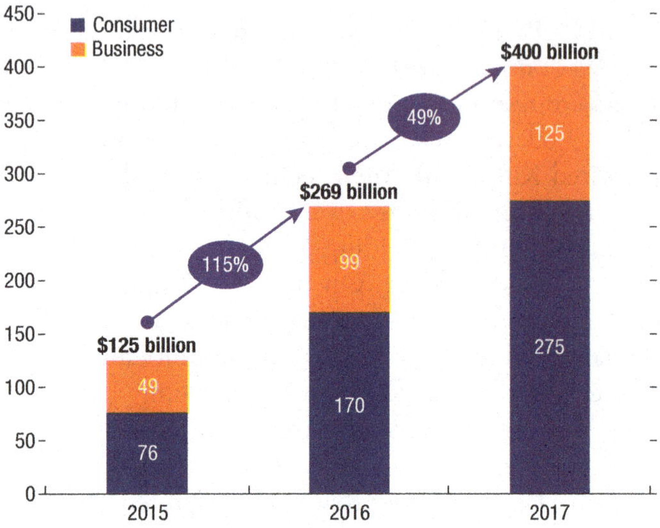

Sources: CCAF; and IMF staff calculations.
Note: Excludes non-sovereign territories. Full data set for emerging and developing Europe, Middle-East and North Africa, and sub-Saharan Africa not available for 2017.

Figure 6. Fintech Credit Composition by Region, 2017
(Percent)

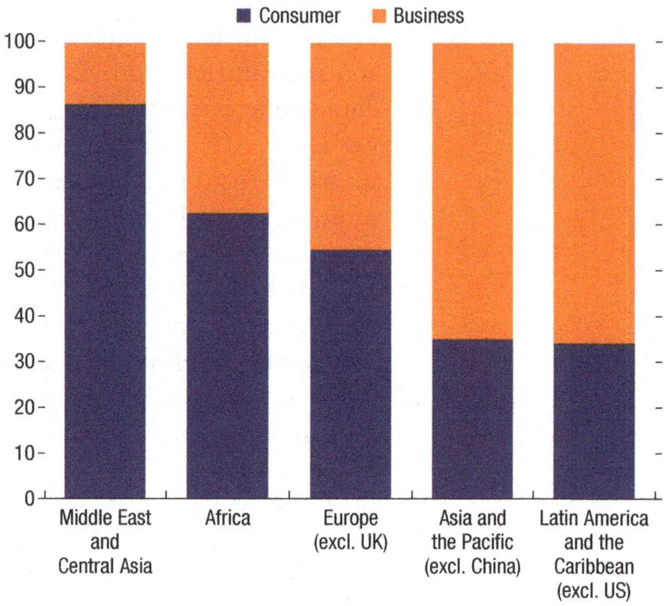

Sources: CCAF; and IMF staff calculations.

Chapter

4 Is Fintech Increasing Financial Inclusion?

There is increasing anecdotal evidence, confirmed through our interviews, that fintech is supporting financial inclusion. Apart from faster speed and higher efficiency that benefits all, we heard from stakeholders that low-income households and SMEs also benefit from lower service cost, little or no collateral requirements for credit extension, and typically better customer experience. Mobile point-of-sale devices are helping SMEs to collect electronic payments, and subsequently use the documented sales as an indicator of creditworthiness to obtain credit. Fintech solutions are also supporting more efficient cash management.

To assess the impact of fintech on financial inclusion beyond the anecdotal evidence, we introduce a new indicator of digital financial inclusion in payments (a description of the methodology is found in Annex 2, and Khera and others, 2020). Using recently available data, we construct two indices. The "digital" financial inclusion index aggregates digital payment services provided through mobile phone and the internet using the methodology in Sahay and others (2015a). The "traditional" financial inclusion index is constructed using the same approach, for financial services provided by traditional financial institutions. The sample covers 52 EMDEs and spans the period 2014–17 for digital financial inclusion and 2011–17 for traditional financial inclusion (Box 1). These indices provide a comprehensive measure of digital financial inclusion across countries before the onset of the COVID-19 crisis.

Digital financial inclusion varies across countries and regions. For instance, the Middle Eastern countries in our sample (green dots in Figure 7) tend to use almost exclusively accounts in financial institutions, while mobile accounts are barely used; conversely, mobile money accounts are generally more present in African countries (red dots). In some African countries, the

Figure 7. Use of Digital and Traditional Financial Accounts, 2017
(Percent)

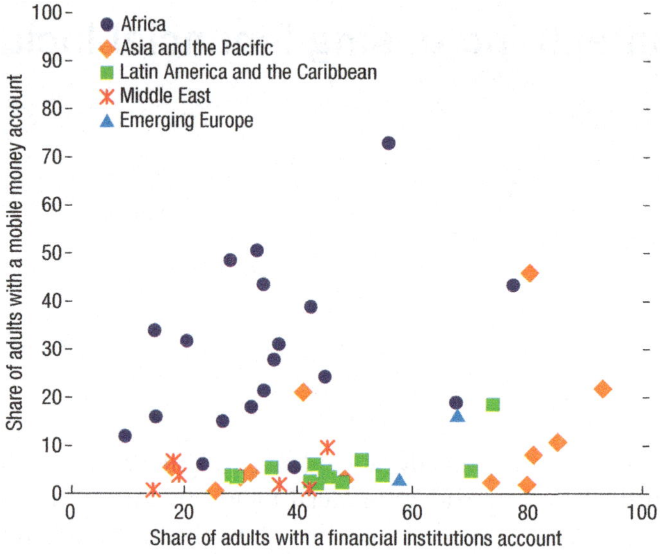

Source: Global Findex.

share of the adult population with mobile account is larger than the share of adults with traditional accounts.

Our index shows that digital financial inclusion has increased significantly in recent years preceding the current crisis. As Figure 8 shows, traditional financial inclusion across the countries in our sample remained broadly unchanged during 2014–17. In the same period, an increasing number of countries have benefitted from digital financial inclusion, as evidenced by the shift and flattening of the distribution to the right.

In some countries, digital financial inclusion appears to have been a game changer.

- Comprehensive financial inclusion (that includes digital and traditional) increased in most countries between 2014 and 2017. As Figure 9 indicates, some countries saw greater progress in digital inclusion (e.g., Benin, Ghana, Senegal), while others in traditional inclusion (e.g., Mongolia, Namibia, Peru).
- In eight cases, including Zimbabwe (where mobile payments have effectively replaced cash transactions), South Africa, and Nigeria, the *progress* in financial inclusion is entirely driven by fintech—the *increase* in digital financial inclusion coincides with a *fall* in the traditional index.

Figure 8. Distribution of Traditional and Digital Financial Inclusion Indices, 2014–17
(Kernel density)

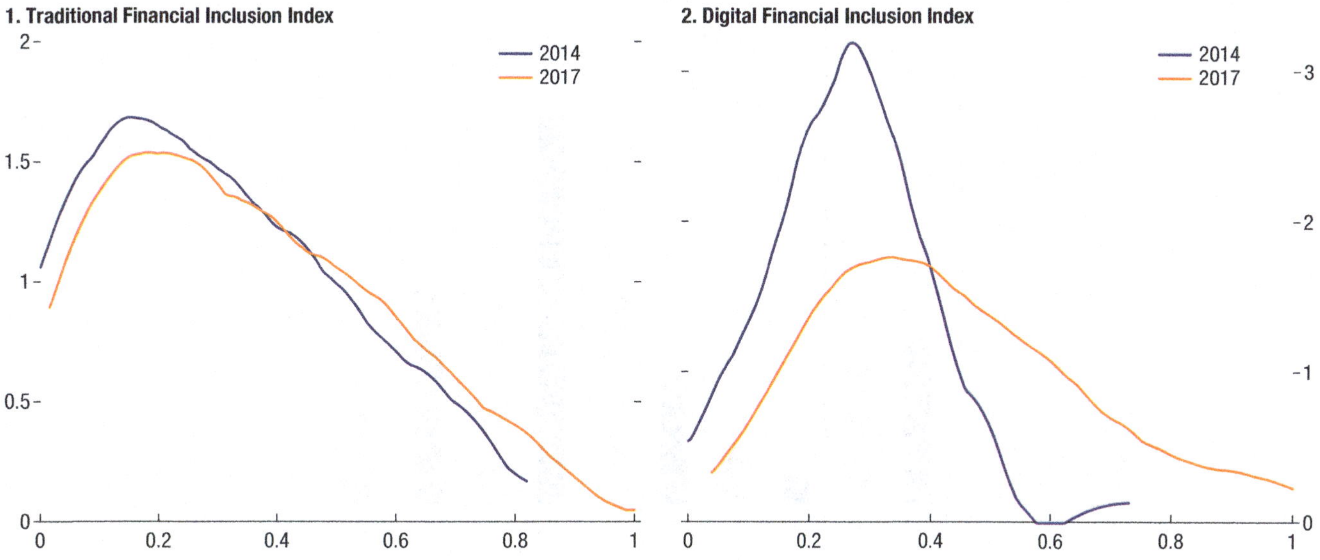

Source: IMF staff calculations (see Annex 2).

Figure 9. Changes in Financial Inclusion Indices, 2014–17
(Level change)

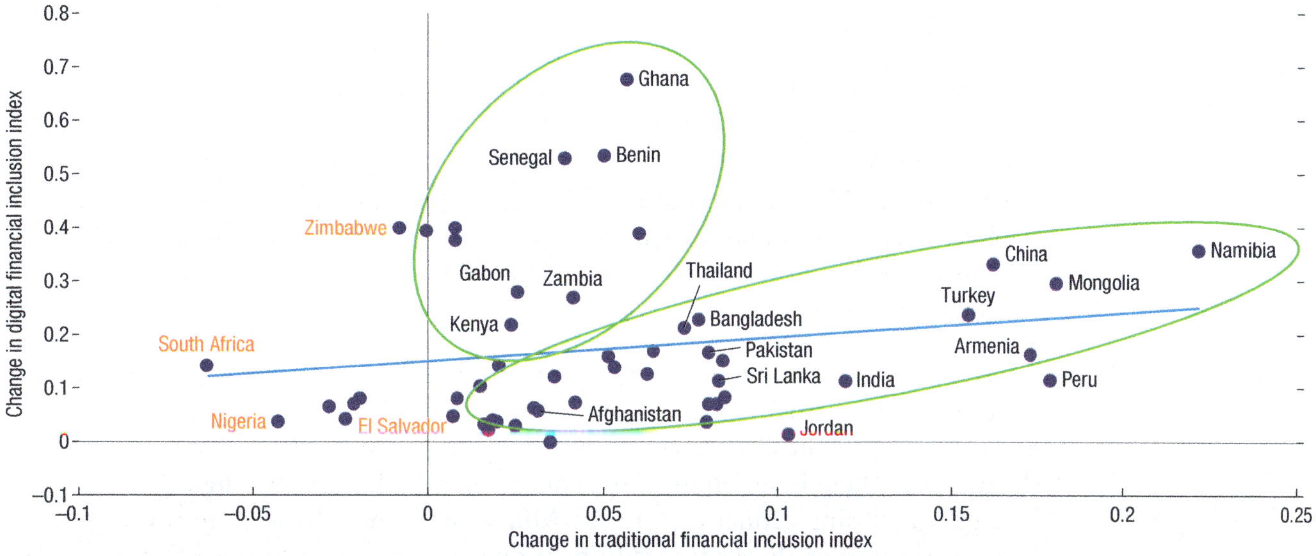

Source: IMF staff calculations (see Annex 2).

Figure 10. Gender Gaps: Traditional versus Fintech-Driven Financial Inclusion, 2017

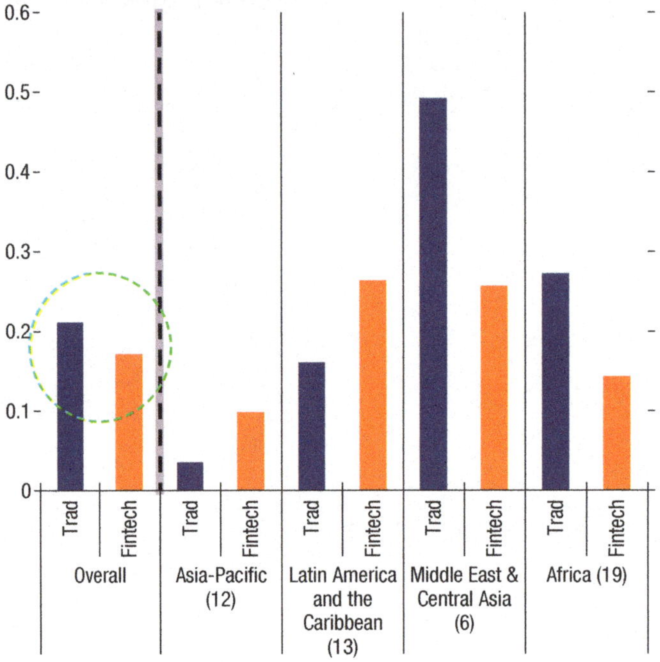

Source: IMF staff calculations (see Appendix 2).
Note: "Trad" is traditional financial inclusion. The gender gap is defined as the percentage difference between the male and female financial inclusion index. Higher values indicate a larger gender gap.

- From a regional perspective, African and Asian countries maintain an overall lead in digital financial inclusion, while in other regions, such as Europe and Latin America, traditional financial inclusion dominates (Box 1).
- There is considerable variation within regions. For instance, in Africa, while Ghana, Kenya, and Uganda are the front runners in digital financial inclusion, other countries such as Nigeria, Madagascar, Republic of the Congo are trailing.

Fintech is contributing toward closing financial inclusion gender gaps, with differences across regions. Gender gaps tend to be slightly lower for fintech-driven financial inclusion than for traditional financial inclusion (Figure 10). There is variation across countries, with fintech playing a positive role in closing gender gaps in the Middle East and African countries. Conversely, gaps are lower for traditional financial inclusion in the Asian and Latin American countries of our sample. Variation across countries may be explained by obstacles that fintech cannot address, such as cultural or social norms, and barriers in financial and digital literacy.

With regard to digital credit, empirical evidence suggests that the quality of infrastructure and the macroeconomic and legal environment help increase access. Using online marketplace lending data for 109 countries over the period 2015–17, we explore the determinants of digital credit extension (Annex 3 describes the methodology and results, with more details in Bazarbash and Beaton 2020).

- Marketplace lending is small and is provided by a relatively large set of lenders. The average size of loans is not available, but the data on average overall credit origination by lending platforms suggests that marketplace lending consists mostly of very small loans, likely to small borrowers (individuals and businesses).
- Marketplace lending fills a gap: it is higher in countries that have less financial depth. In addition, better credit information, a larger access to the internet, and stronger legal rights are also associated with larger digital lending: in other words, marketplace lending requires a sufficiently developed environment to thrive.

In the long-term, the COVID-19 pandemic has the potential to accelerate progress in digital financial inclusion, and anecdotal evidence suggests it is already happening. The SARS epidemic in 2003 accelerated China's launching of digital payments and e-commerce (World Economic Forum).[1] Hence, we can expect to see higher digital financial inclusion across the globe post COVID-19. In fact, in many countries it is already happening. For example, mobile money transactions increased by 450 percent between January and April 2020 in Rwanda (ranked high in our digital financial inclusion index), and the number of users sending money virtually doubled from 0.6 million in the week before lockdown to 1.2 million in the week after lockdown, and to 1.8 million in the final week of April (Rwanda Utilities Regulation Authority).[2] This is also corroborated by recent research which shows that the spread of the COVID-19 has led to a statistically significant increase in adoption of fintech, proxied by mobile finance-based application downloads (Fu and Mishra 2020).[3]

In the short term, however, the divide in the progress in digital financial inclusion across and within countries could widen. Developing digital infrastructure takes resources and time, which would make it difficult for countries with low access to digital financial inclusion to scale up quickly given the priority they need to give to spending on health and economic support more broadly (para 59). On the other hand, countries with already high

[1]https://www.weforum.org/agenda/2020/05/digital-payments-cash-and-COVID-19-pandemics/

[2]https://rura.rw/index.php?id=23

[3]The download of finance mobile application is estimated to have increased by 24 percent on average across 74 countries since the start of the lockdown, compared to prior trends.

access to digital financial services would likely be able to accelerate its adoption even further—both because of the potentially higher demand and related supportive measures implemented by authorities.[4]

[4]In the short-term, there could be two opposing impacts of COVID-19 on demand for digital payments: on one hand, it would increase as people favor digital and contactless payments to comply with social distancing measures, in parallel with the shift towards e-commerce; on the other hand, people might curb spending and hence use of digital payments due to staying indoors, fall in incomes, and loss of employment.

Box 1. Measuring Fintech-Driven (Digital) Financial Inclusion

One of the key contributions of this paper is the introduction of a novel financial inclusion index (see Figure 1.1.1). It combines a traditional (bank-based) and a digital financial inclusion component and covers 52 EMDEs. The measure combines indicators of access to and usage of traditional and digital payments services, such as ATM and bank branches, mobile and internet access, account holding, and usage of financial institutions/mobile account for wage and utility payments. A comprehensive financial inclusion index is constructed using a three-stage principal component analysis: the first stage combines various indicators to compute measures of "access" to and "usage" of payment services, separately for both traditional and digital financial inclusion; the second stage computes "traditional financial inclusion" and "digital financial inclusion" indices combining the respective access and usage indicators from the first stage; and lastly traditional and digital financial inclusion indices are combined to build comprehensive financial inclusion index of a country.[1]

Figure 1.1.1. Financial Inclusion Index

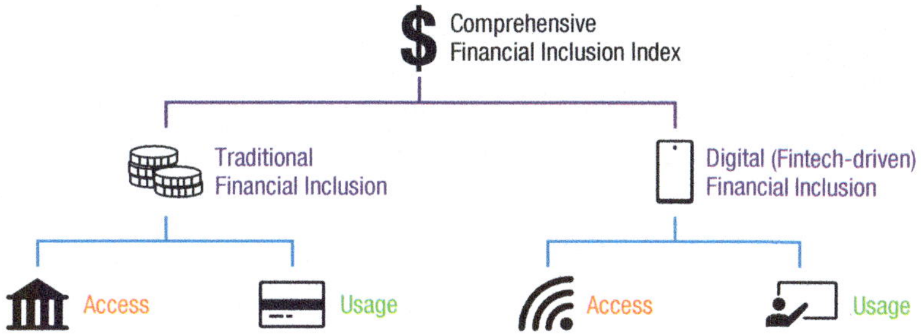

Source: IMF staff.

The addition of indicators related to digital payments services expands the scope of the measurement of financial inclusion in the existing literature. Figure 1.1.2 displays the index by region.

The new financial inclusion index has limitations. Due to lack of comparable data, the index only covers 52 EMDEs. The raw data does not distinguish between digital services provided by fintech companies or banks, which precludes an analysis of whether fintech companies are competing with or complementing the services provided by traditional financial institutions.

[1]See Annex 2 for technical detail. Data sources include IMF Financial Access Survey, World Bank Global Findex Database, and GSMA.

Box 1. Measuring Fintech-Driven (Digital) Financial Inclusion *(continued)*

Figure 1.1.2. Digital Financial Inclusion Index, 2014–17

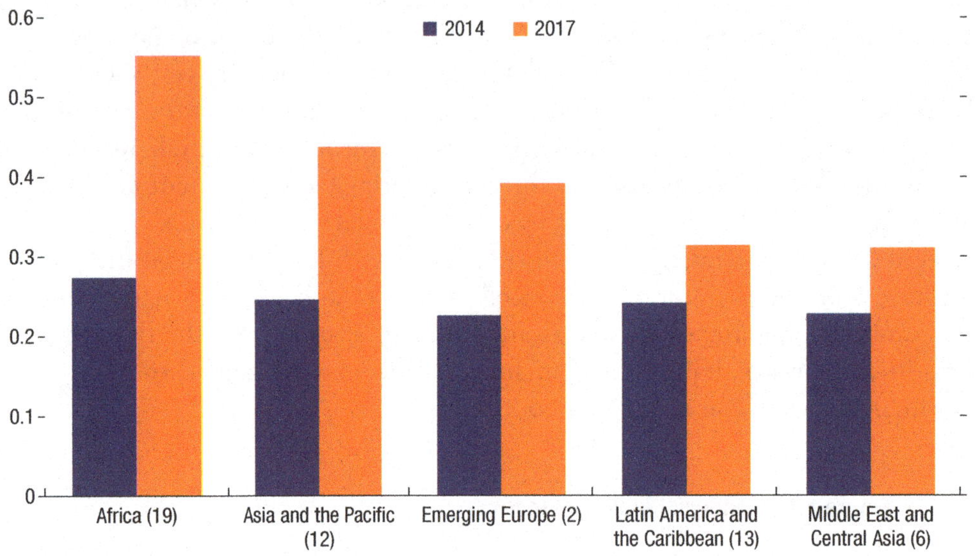

Source: IMF staff calculations (see Annex 2).

CHAPTER

5 What Are the Macroeconomic Implications?

The positive macroeconomic impact of financial inclusion is well documented, both theoretically and empirically. Sahay and others (2015a) and Čihák and Sahay (2020) show that both financial access and financial deepening support growth and lower income inequality, with limited negative externalities on financial stability as long as the regulatory environment is sound. Loukoianova and Yang (2018) also point to growth benefits from financial inclusion. However, financial inclusion of less productive agents can also negatively affect growth (Dabla-Norris and others 2015b).

Our empirical work finds that in the recent years, payment services have had a stronger association with growth where financial inclusion was driven by fintech. We examine the drivers of real GDP growth over 2014–18 and 2011–18 in the sample of 52 countries for which we have computed digital financial inclusion indices, using standard cross-country OLS regressions (Annex 4 and Khera and others 2020). To identify the impact of digital financial inclusion on growth, we relate the initial levels of traditional and digital financial inclusion to subsequent average growth, along with a standard set of country-level control variables. Initial values are used to reduce biases stemming from reverse causation.[1] The results point to the following conclusions:

- Digital financial inclusion is significantly positively associated with growth, consistent with the notion that fintech might contribute to growth, while traditional financial inclusion does not (Figure 11). This difference may be that the impact from traditional financial inclusion has already been reaped

[1]To establish a robust causal link between growth in digital financial inclusion and GDP growth, identifying a valid instrument for change in digital financial inclusion over the time span of GDP growth will help overcome potential biases stemming from endogeneity or reverse causation. This is explored more in detail in Khera and others (2020).

Figure 11. Impact of Digital Financial Inclusion in Payments on Growth
(Percent of annual GDP growth)

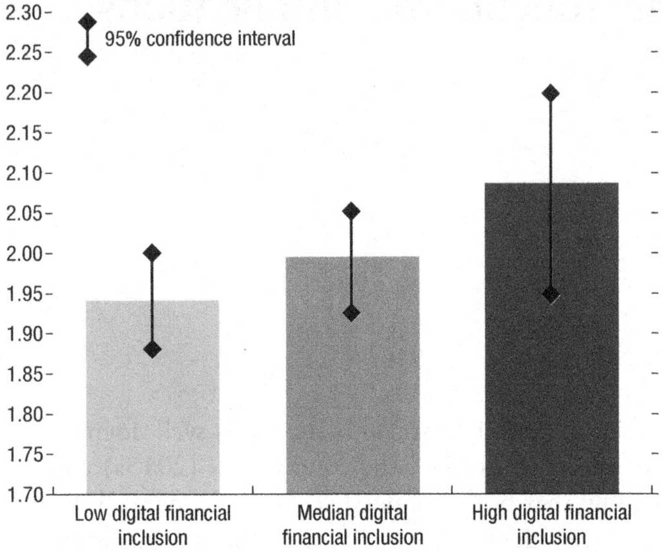

Source: IMF staff calculations (see Annexes 2 and 4).
Note: Using the coefficient estimates obtained from the regression, annual GDP growth rates for countries with low (25th percentile), median, and high (75th percentile) levels of financial inclusion were calculated, holding other explanatory factors at their median levels.

prior to the period covered in the analysis, whereas the benefits of digital financial inclusion have only just started.

- This result could reflect the positive impact of the use of digital payments on transaction costs, liquidity, and creditworthiness (Islam, Muzi, and Rodriguez Meza 2018). Since our analysis only captures payments and does not cover several components of digital finance (savings, credit, and insurance), it is likely to underestimate the impact on growth. That said, the impact of digital credit on sustainable growth will depend on its ability to finance longer-term investment—which remains an open question.

These findings suggest that digital financial inclusion could play an important role in mitigating the economic impact of the COVID-19 crisis and helping the recovery, provided pre-conditions for accelerating digital services exist. Some studies have found that digital financial inclusion can help dampen economic shocks and smooth consumption (Jack and Suri 2014). While the effect of digital financial inclusion on economic activity during and beyond the COVID-19 shock is yet to be examined, the ability of fintech to help cope with the crisis and in the recovery will likely depend on (1) the extent of digital financial inclusion at the onset of the COVID-19 crisis (see above); (2) the ability to quickly scale up digital financial inclusion, i.e., availability of enabling factors and policies needed for digital financial services; (3) pre-existing regulatory and supervisory gaps that could amplify risks; and (4) fintech sector's resilience and changes in its landscape during the economic downturn. The latter three factors are explored in the sections that follow.

CHAPTER

6 Are Fintech Companies Disrupting Traditional Providers?

The fintech companies that target the under- and unserved populations have had a limited disruptive impact on traditional bank operations so far. The services that fintech companies are providing (for instance, small loans at short duration or aggregator of services of various companies on their digital platform) are typically not services that traditional banks provide to small clients. The 24/7 access to online lending platforms is allowing small SMEs to seek financing outside of business hours. In some sense, the fintech companies are complementing the services of traditional providers who focus on big clients and larger loans for longer duration. In advanced economies, for instance, where fintech lenders target the underserved borrowers, fintech companies do not compete with the broad spectrum of services provided by banks, but rather provide "pointed technical solutions" in niche areas.

Interviews with fintech companies suggest that they are increasingly collaborating with banks and creating a variety of business models. Fintech companies are partnering with banks to benefit from their experience and expertise in regulatory compliance and to facilitate scaling up. In turn, fintech companies provide banks with the state-of-the-art platform for reaching out to new customers. In some cases, especially in EMDEs, digital microcredit is operated by fintech companies that manage the lending on behalf of the banks. Big banks are also inviting fintech companies to set up in-house incubator and innovation labs (for example, Barclays and Lloyds). In Korea, which has a very high penetration of credit cards, some fintech companies offer platforms that serve as aggregators and connectors to the services provided by credit card companies.

The limited disruption of traditional providers so far, and the complementarity between fintech and banks, is also confirmed in our empirical work. Indeed, digital solutions appear to be "filling the gap" left by traditional financial institutions (Annexes 3 and 5).

Figure 12. Tech Spending in Fintech, 2019
(US$ billion)

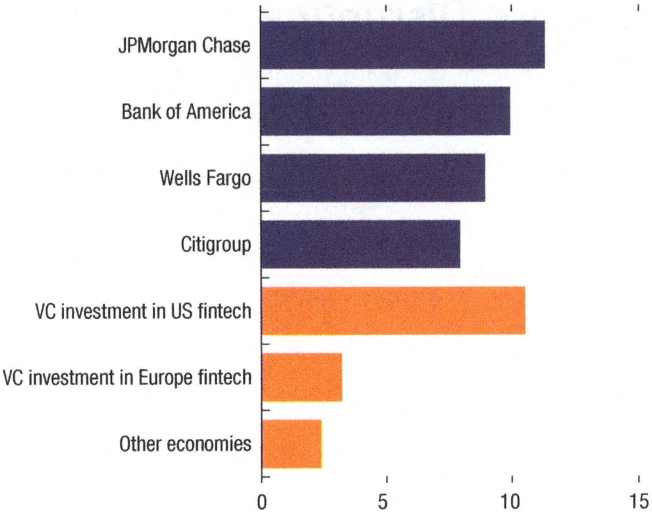

Source: Bank disclosures, data compiled by Faux, 2020, KPMG Pulse of Fintech Report & Innovate Finance Investment landscape report, based on Pitchbook Data. Note: Venture capital (VC) investment data based on 2018 levels. Other economies include Brazil, Canada, Hong Kong SAR, India, and Japan.

- Fintech payment services tend to be supplied more, and used more, where traditional access is limited. Our work on digital payments show that the availability of traditional means of financial inclusion (such as access to bank branches and ATMs) is negatively associated with both the supply and usage of digital payments. While this may in part reflect the shift by banks toward digital means of service provision (e.g., mobile and online banking), it suggests that digital financial inclusion tends to be higher where there is a gap in the existing supply of traditional financial services or when the traditional banking sector is inefficient.
- Fintech credit also tends to emerge where traditional services are limited, i.e., where bank branches are few, and financial depth is lower.

That said, competition between traditional and nontraditional providers, though nascent, is emerging. For instance, purely digital banks are coming up, directly competing for traditional bank customers and attracting new ones due to their technological advantages and low-cost services. Similarly, fintech lenders now compete directly with informal money lenders, microfinance institutions, and small banks in both payment and credit. Big banks, too, are beginning to feel the competitive pressure and are responding in different ways. Some are buying up small fintech companies or investing heavily in fintech—their combined investment in 2018 overtook investment by venture capitalists in fintech companies (Figure 12). This trend could be further strengthened as they adopt to lockdowns and social distancing measures to contain the COVID-19 pandemic by accelerating the shift toward digital delivery services.

CHAPTER

7 What Are the Factors that Enable and Constrain Digital Financial Inclusion?

The literature and our interviews with stakeholders highlight several enabling factors for financial inclusion. These include customer identification, digital infrastructure, financial literacy, and a supportive regulatory and legal environment for making progress in digital financial inclusion.

Customer identification is a first step for promoting financial inclusion (AFI 2018). Financial services require accurate identification of customers, including to prevent fraudulent activities. Many creative solutions are emerging: in EMDEs, telephone numbers are often used as a source of identification for providing basic services such as payments; countries are developing centralized database for customer due diligence identification. In some advanced economies, fintech companies are working with regulatory authorities (such as the Financial Conduct Authority in the United Kingdom.) to set up "digital portable identity" in order to help small businesses expand rapidly. These digital identities can be stored in smart phones and used across institutions and borders. The introduction of the Aadhaar card in India, a national system of biometric identification issued to more than 1 billion people, has been a game changer. Its potential usage is high, ranging from delivering national services (pension, health, insurance, and social welfare payments) to digital financial services to satisfying regulatory requirements on customers' identity.[1] Biometric identification has also been introduced in developing Pacific countries, such as Papua New Guinea or Samoa, allowing unregistered persons to use fintech-based payments. A key regulatory and legal issue in many countries is to balance between information sharing and privacy protection.

Interviews with fintech companies highlighted two major constraints: uncertainty of the regulatory environment and lack of technological expertise—the

[1]For instance, customer due diligence requirements are critical for correspondent banking purposes, and therefore for remittances.

"coders." Interviewees noted that uncertainty or frequent changes in the regulatory environment was, in some sense, more of a constraint than a clear road map with tighter regulation. In some countries, the regulatory support measures, implemented as a response to the COVID-19 shock, are designed to be channeled mainly through the banking sector, which could further exacerbate these constraints. The shortage of technological expertise, the coders, is also increasingly weighing on their minds, particularly in EMDEs. Further, although many fintech firms rely on alternative data to assess creditworthiness, they thought credit bureaus could help augment their assessments. Fintech firms seeking to expand globally also noted the lack of universal credit scores and legal frameworks for loan recovery as impediments.

Funding constraints, especially to scale-up, were also mentioned by many fintech companies, and is even more evident during the COVID-19 crisis. Initial support or funding typically comes through incubators or accelerator programs or from angel investors and crowdfunding. Some are increasingly being funded through private equity, venture capital, and hedge funds, while a few successful ones are already being publicly listed on stock exchanges. Both interviews and preliminary data suggest that funding constraints have become increasingly acute during the COVID-19 shock, particularly for those firms with thin liquidity and capital buffers. Fintech funding activity stalled in the first quarter of 2020 across regions: for instance, Asia saw a 69 percent drop in funding and a 23 percent drop in deals quarter-over-quarter.[2]

Regulatory authorities we spoke with noted the wide-ranging challenges they are facing. These included catching up with the fast-changing landscape, facing budgetary constraints or lack of expertise, and managing lobbying pressures from traditional financial institutions. Regulators are also responding to the development of fintech by encouraging and adopting RegTech (The use of information technologies (IT) to enhance regulatory processes) and SupTech (the use of IT to enhance supervision). From the financial service providers perspective, the automation and data-driven analysis of internal control systems and reporting are enhancing cost-efficiency. From the supervisors' perspective, it allows for risk-based supervision of vast amounts of data. According to one RegTech company, the cost of compliance for one of their clients went down from £18 million to £0.5 million per annum by switching to their technology.

The lack of financial literacy or non-familiarity with new technology was often mentioned as a constraint on the demand side, which is limiting the outreach of COVID-19 related economic support to the most needy. Interestingly, stakeholders in both advanced and EMDEs noted the low level of

[2]https://www.cbinsights.com/research/report/fintech-trends-q1-2020/

Figure 13. Marginal Effect of Digital Infrastructures and Financial Familiarity on Digital Financial Inclusion, 2014–17

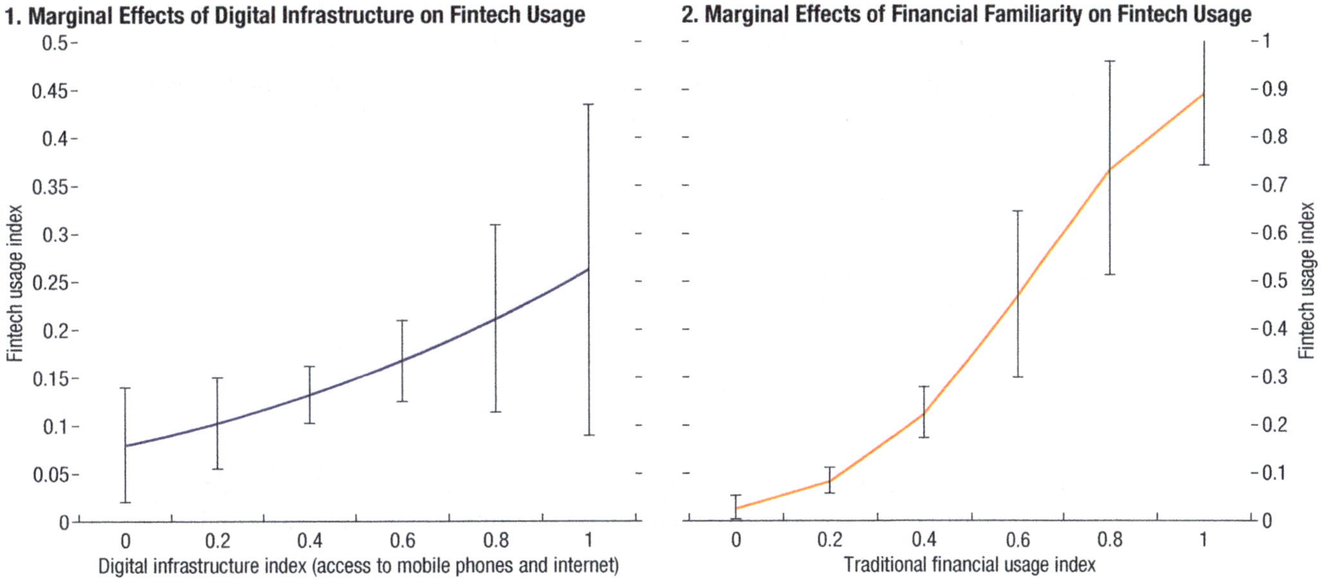

Source: IMF staff calculations (see Annexes 2 and 5).
Note: The charts indicate the expected mean level of digital usage index, conditional on the level of digital infrastructure and traditional financial usage indices. Conditional means are calculated based on pooled regressions using the data for 2014 and 2017, holding other explanatory factors at their mean level.

financial literacy of their customers. Several fintech companies have added tutorials on their website to enable the learning of basic concepts. Singaporean authorities have taken wide-ranging initiatives to educate their population. However, interviews with fintech companies revealed that lack of access to e-government in several countries during the COVID-19 crisis is proving to be a major constraint to reach the most needy.

Our empirical work identifies factors that facilitate or impede digital financial inclusion.

- Our analysis (Annex 5) shows that better access to digital infrastructure (measured by the availability of the internet and mobile phones) is associated with higher usage of digital payments and credit (Figure 13). In fact, we find a monotonic and positive relationship at all levels of digital infrastructure. Similarly, increasing the number of mobile money agents in the same proportion would also lead to improvements in digital financial inclusion (although the magnitude would be smaller).
- The efficiency of traditional providers also matters. More inefficient banking systems (with higher overhead costs to total assets) are associated with more digital financial inclusion.

- The usage of fintech payment services is higher where there is already a high usage of traditional financial services. This could reflect higher financial literacy, as well as trust in the financial system in general.[3]
- Institutions matter, at least for the development of mobile money agents, and the quality of governance is positively associated with the availability of mobile money agents.
- Finally, a more consumer-friendly environment (i.e., higher mobile money regulation index) is, as expected, associated with greater adoption of mobile money.
- On the credit side, our work on marketplace lending indicates that the availability of borrower information and higher protection of legal rights tend to support the emergence and development of fintech credit (Annex 3).

The priorities in promoting digital financial inclusion should depend on country circumstances. For example, for countries where traditional access is low, there is room to improve financial inclusion through fintech, irrespective of the level of usage. Conversely, for countries where traditional usage is low, enhancing financial literacy and, more broadly, familiarity with financial services, is essential to support financial inclusion, irrespective of access.

The experience with the COVID-19 crisis underscores the importance of promoting digital services to the most needy. Fiscal policy should include investment in digital infrastructure such as access to electricity, mobile, and internet coverage, digital ID among others (IMF 2020a). In some countries where digital access is higher, the crisis could provide the needed push to accelerate initiatives already in the pipeline in areas related to building conducive regulatory and institutional frameworks. These efforts should be complemented by the promotion of consumer and data protection, cybersecurity, interoperability, and financial and digital literacy.

[3]This could also reflect complementarities between mobile banking and formal traditional banking; for instance, in many sub-Saharan African countries mobile financial services have to be backed by a formal bank account.

CHAPTER

8 What Are the Risks of Fintech to Financial Inclusion?

Regulators around the globe have begun to assess the fintech-related risks and formulate policies, and these should be accelerated during and after the COVID-19 crisis. At the international level, the Financial Stability Board (FSB) has concluded that fintech and Big Tech do not yet present systemic risks (FSB 2017, 2019). At the same time, it is worth recalling that the push for financial inclusion without proper regulation contributed to the 2008 global financial crisis. The development of digital lending is already raising concerns about predatory lending practices in some countries, which could become even more prevalent in the ongoing COVID-19 crisis (Faux 2020). For instance, fintech borrowers who are unable to make loan repayments due to sudden loss of income, might be subject to aggressive debt collection practices and high late payment/default fees. In Indonesia, the Financial Services Authority has identified and closed down more than 1,000 illegal peer-to-peer lenders recently that were offering prohibited financial services or operating without a proper license. Therefore, a sound policy approach at both the global and domestic level is crucial (IMF 2019a). Global cooperation is needed to mitigate risks related to the possible emergence of global monopolies such as the Big Techs, regulatory arbitrage and race to the bottom, cross-border activities, cybersecurity, and money laundering (IMF 2019b, 2018a). At the domestic level, the list is also long: it includes protecting data; preventing cyber risk (UK Financial Conduct Authority 2018); facilitating digital infrastructure; strengthening regulatory and supervisory frameworks; upgrading payment and securities settlement systems; ensuring standardization and interoperability; and developing effective user protection and contingency planning.

Risks that fintech might pose to financial inclusion itself—both digital and traditional—have been much less explored. The risks mentioned above were also present in the mind of the stakeholders we interviewed. But, as discussed below, the extent to which fintech could put financial inclusion itself at risk has been much less explored to date.

Could Fintech Create Direct Risks to Financial Inclusion?

Reaping the benefits of fintech requires a minimum level of investment and those who do not have the means may find themselves financially excluded. Investment here includes "tech capital" (e.g., mobile phones, internet access) as well as the human capital required to use digital financial services. As fintech develops and becomes more sophisticated, uneven access to the needed physical infrastructure, or insufficient human capital, could create a new source of financial exclusion, notably among women, the poor, and the elderly, in both EMDEs and advanced economies (G20 2019). The COVID-19 shock has induced a strong shift toward digital financial services, a trend that could exacerbate financial exclusion of those groups left behind. Moreover, "easy" digital credit creates risks for people with limited financial literacy (Kaffenberger, Totolo, and Soursourian 2018).

The use of big data analytics could become a source of financial exclusion if the initial data entry is biased, or if algorithms are imperfectly calibrated. Fintech firms' use of big data and algorithms to profile consumers can allow them to reach customers who, until then, had been excluded from the traditional financial sector because of no or limited credit history (Bazarbash 2019). But there are concerns that it may also entrench biases present in historical data, and this in turn could perpetuate the unfair treatment—and exclusion—of some categories of consumers. While the concern is present everywhere, the issue has been mostly studied in the case of digital lending in the United States, where disparate treatment and fair lending violations on the basis of customers' characteristics has been identified as a risk (Jagtiani and Lemieux 2017; FinRegLab 2019). Furthermore, the unprecedented economic impact brought by the COVID-19 shock will likely test the reliability of existing models and indicators in the downturn, potentially requiring adjustments and recalibrations. The Financial Action Task Force (FATF) standard on ML/TF promotes a risk-based approach that encourages countries to design measures that meet the national goal of financial inclusion without undermining the measures that exist for fighting ML/TF. However, an improper or disproportionate implementation of the risk-based approach to ML/TF, including through the use of big data analytics, may aggravate financial exclusion (e.g., blanket exclusion of categories of customers associated with higher risks of terrorist financing).

Financial inclusion through fintech could be more procyclical than financial inclusion through traditional means, as is already being observed in some regions following the COVID-19 crisis. The small size of fintech credit limits the potential impact of a fintech credit cycle on the economy. But fintech lending is growing rapidly, in part because the automation of credit decisions makes credit extension more frequent and much faster. Insofar as credit provision based on large and frequently updated datasets allows for a robust evaluation of creditworthiness, such credit could be resilient to the economic cycle. At the same time, automation could also lead to procyclicality—to the extent that algorithms do not substitute for long-term relationship with clients, more automated credit decisions could also lead to faster contraction during a downturn (Carstens 2018). The procyclicality could further be exacerbated by the tightening of funding conditions of fintech lenders, as some are starting to experience during the current health crisis. Many of these firms are new and less established, with less liquidity and balance sheet buffers. They could retrench their operations more sharply in downturns, curtailing access to financial services for SMEs and low-income households disproportionately.[1] If this results in consolidation, the fintech industry could become more concentrated with a few large firms emerging as dominant players. Finally, where fintech (and Big Tech) companies intermediate small deposits, banks funding structure may become more dependent on wholesale deposits, which could be more volatile. Swings in bank funding could lead to contraction in credit, with could be particularly detrimental to the marginal borrowers. Altogether, these effects could lead to procyclical swings in financial inclusion.

Could Fintech Create Indirect Risks to Financial Inclusion?

As fintech develops, the microfinance institutions and small banks that have traditionally catered to the financially vulnerable may suffer. Some of those financial institutions—including, in many cases, the traditional money lenders in low-income countries—embraced the digital transformation early on, collaborating with fintech companies. But the pressure from fintech could put the business models of the laggards at risk: digital credit and saving solutions, fully online banks, or money transfer solutions are making inroads into some of their business lines. These institutions have less resources to respond to competitive pressures they face from nimble fintech companies. If they were to scale back their operations before fintech companies have sufficiently scaled up, the risk of financial exclusion could increase. The COVID-19 crisis could increase this risk: in addition to their clients being likely to be hit harder by the economic fallout of the pandemic, many microfinance institutions lack the expertise and resources to expand digital operations at least in the near term.

[1]There is already some evidence of this happening in some countries, such as in Indonesia: https://www.ft.com/content/8992491e-8c83-4b02-81a6-b122a0633918?shareType=nongift

A loss of trust in digital technologies could setback progress in financial inclusion. The progress in digital financial inclusion rests on the delicate balance of convenience provided by the technology and trust placed by customers in fintech. For instance, the increased availability of personal data can play an important role in facilitating identification of the people most adversely impacted by the COVID-19 crisis, such as by mobile wallet providers in China and Kenya. However, loopholes or fraud in the handling of private data can erode trust. Data privacy or cyber security concerns might prompt consumers to look for ways to reduce fintech companies' access to their data, thereby reducing the ability of fintech to support financial inclusion. Recognizing these risks, some regulators noted that a code-of-conduct directive for fintech firms was in order, especially those dealing with retail customers.

Inadequate user protection could also undermine digital financial inclusion. Households must trust that mobile money or e-wallets are a reliable means of payment. However, risks exist. The mobile money operator could go bankrupt. Alternatively, the bank holding its funds as deposits (which are the aggregation of mobile money users' funds) could fail. In these scenarios, mobile money users may not fully recover their balances. However, some of these risks can be mitigated. Legal structures ensuring the segregation of customer funds from other creditors of the mobile money operator should be explored. Also, customer funds should be invested in highly safe and liquid assets and should be diversified across the safest banks to the extent they are held as deposits of the mobile money operator. Another option is for central banks to require that mobile money operators hold customer funds as central bank reserves.[2]

[2]China, Peru, the Philippines, and Thailand require that the e-float be deposited at the central bank. Adrian and Mancini-Griffoli (2019) refer to this scheme more generally as synthetic CBDC (sCBDC for short). sCBDC is a public-private partnership allowing the private sector to interact with customers and innovate on the technological front, while central banks regulate the system and ultimately provide trust.

CHAPTER

9 Future Agenda

As fintech develops, policymakers are facing questions relevant for inclusive growth, financial stability, and regulation. The G20 has identified the need to "provide an enabling and proportionate legal and regulatory framework for digital financial inclusion" as one if its High-Level Principles for Digital Financial Inclusion (G20 2016), and there is an active effort by all stakeholders, including think tanks, to think through the contribution of regulation to the safe development of fintech which preserves financial integrity (Staschen and Meagher 2018). This is an important point, as fintech is often allowing the development of unregulated substitutes to highly regulated activities, such as currency issuance or consumer finance. Currently, there are no internationally agreed regulatory standards, but country authorities around the globe are responding, with China, India, Mexico, Singapore, and the United Kingdom, among the countries that are taking a more proactive role. The United Nations Secretary-General's Special Advocate for Inclusive Finance for Development (UNSGSA 2019) identifies several preconditions for raising digital financial inclusion safely and competitively. These include data privacy, cybersecurity, digital identification, fair competition, physical infrastructure (agents network, connectivity, interoperability), and financial and digital literacy. Though a tall order, it provides a clear set of goals for policymakers to pursue.

In this context, ensuring high-quality supervision and regulation, particularly of nonbank financial institutions is important. Supervisors have recognized the need to adapt regulatory approaches that strike the right balance between enabling financial innovation and addressing challenges and risks to financial integrity, consumer protection, and financial stability. Examples include the adoption of mechanisms such as innovation hubs and, where appropriate, regulatory sandboxes. Importantly, regulation should remain proportionate to the risks and should support the safe use of innovative technologies (Taylor and others 2020).

It is becoming imperative that international agreements are needed to address data privacy, cybersecurity, cross-border digital currencies, and digital identification. A valuable benefit of fintech: it offers the ability to conduct transactions securely and cheaply. But it is important to guard against misuse, such as ML/TF. Some progress is in the works: for instance, the FATF has revised its standards to respond to the real risks that the use of virtual assets can pose. But developing other standards will be difficult, given large differences across countries on what such standards should entail (for instance, national preferences regarding information sharing and data privacy can diverge widely).[1]

International agreements are also needed related to anti-trust laws to ensure adequate competition in the fintech and overall financial services sector. Big Tech firms such as Alibaba, Amazon, Apple, Facebook, Google, and Tencent bring value in terms of speed, efficiency, and economies of scale. At the same time, with their global footprint and funding advantages, they could easily put smaller companies out of business and be formidable competitors to established financial institutions. With an abundance of cash and business lines that fit well with the COVID-19 demands, Big Techs are doubling down on acquisitions and research and development.[2] With smaller companies being hard hit by the tighter funding conditions, it is important to ensure that the fintech landscape remains sufficiently competitive after the COVID-19 crisis. Furthermore, the entry of Big Tech companies is raising questions from a number of perspectives (loss of sovereignty, cost of global monopolies, and others). On the policy side, there is a concern that small countries and their regulatory policies could ultimately be captured by these giants.

Financial and digital literacy is as much of a scarcity in advanced economies as in EMDEs. Emerging markets with younger populations seem to be adapting to fintech much better than aging advanced economies. But common across regions is the fact that few countries mandate courses in financial literacy in high school or college. One country official in an emerging market reported introducing such a course as a high school graduation requirement, but then pointed out that they quickly ran out of teachers who had the qualifications or experience to teach high school students. Challenges for countries with larger populations, remote regions, or cultural resistance to the use of digital communication means, remain immense. Authorities should undertake measures to increase financial and digital literacy, including through creating incentives for private digital service providers to educate customers.

[1]See Carrière-Swallow and Haksar (2019) for a discussion of the risks posed by international fragmentation of data policies, and the need for dialogue and cooperation to avoid such an outcome.

[2]In the first quarter of 2020, total research and development spending at five big Big Techs—Amazon, Facebook, Apple, Alphabet, and Microsoft — increased by 17 percent from the first quarter of 2019.

There are also several macrofinancial risks related to fintech that need to be addressed. Fintech adds to the interconnectedness of the financial system and brings banks and (often unregulated) nonbanks even closer, posing risks for both. Even when fintech companies are unleveraged, they could be affected by spillovers from turbulences in the banking or capital markets. And that, in turn, could put financial inclusion at risk. Finally, fintech could lead to "excessive" financial inclusion (such as the US subprime lending crisis or the more recent rise in default rate to nearly 20 percent on mobile bank loans in Kenya) when access to credit grows under insufficient regulation and supervision.[3] In crafting new laws, it would be important to ensure proportionality in regulation of small fintech firms (Adrian and Mancini-Griffoli 2019), while being mindful that unsecured digital credit combined with the light regulation of some digital financial service providers may raise complex issues of crisis management. These issues are even more relevant as fintech companies go through the economic downturn triggered by the pandemic. For instance, individuals may seek fast access to credit, including digital credit, to meet immediate living expenses. This practice may expose consumers to less scrupulous credit providers, unfavorable terms and conditions, and increase over-indebtedness.

Fintech's potential to help counter the impact of the COVID-19 pandemic and support the eventual economic recovery is large but cannot be taken for granted. Fintech is proving to be a useful tool in ensuring access to financial services and helping deliver governments' support measures. Its role in the recovery phase, however, will depend on the industry's resilience to the shock and how the fintech landscape evolves post-COVID-19. As more date becomes available, it would be useful to examine the relationship between the adoption of digital financial services and how well economies are absorbing the COVID-19 shock and recovering post-COVID.

Are digital financial services closing gender gaps? Women face multiple obstacles in accessing finance, including because of lower literacy and numeracy, lack of documentation, family responsibilities, or social attitudes (Sioson and Kim 2019). Although some of those obstacles may also affect men, they tend to be more important for women. Fintech solutions appear particularly well adapted to the constraints women face—the interfaces are being increasingly designed to be consumer-friendly and digital finance does not require physical presence to access financial services (Jack and Suri 2016). When a face-to-face interaction is needed, e.g., to cash in or cash out, mobile money or bank agents are easily accessible. The AFI identified leveraging digital financial services as one of the top action points to address gender gaps in

[3]Excessive financial deepening is also connected to inequality (Čihák and Sahay (2020); the IMF MD's speech in January 2020: https://www.imf.org/en/News/Articles/2020/01/17/sp01172019-the-financial-sector-in-the-2020s#_edn7).

financial inclusion (AFI 2017). A forthcoming IMF study is looking at the evidence on fintech in bridging gender gaps (Khera and others 2020).

A final thought for policymakers is whether fintech for financial inclusion requires additional consideration from a political economy perspective. GDP growth, notwithstanding its limitation, is currently viewed as the leading indicator for measuring the well-being of an economy. But should there be equal concern if new technology, such as fintech, does not serve large segments of the lower-income society, even if the positive impact on GDP is large? Minimizing the risks of fintech to financial exclusion takes a new meaning if the political cost and social implications of ignoring the "small guy" is high, evidenced by the social unrest in many countries during the COVID-19 crisis. Indeed, high or rising inequalities of income and wealth, in part attributed to new technology, is becoming a major source of concern in a number of countries, which will likely exacerbate during the post COVID-19 era, unless financial exclusion is addressed. The silver lining is that—with careful regulation and supervision, as well as addressing the several constraints that the expansion of financial inclusion faces—countries can attain the promise of fintech to serve greater proportions of the population in realizing their dreams of upward mobility.

Annex 1. Outreach and Interviews

We conducted interviews with more than 50 companies, focusing on regions and countries in which fintech companies are active. The companies vary in size and activity (e.g., payments, credit, insurance, and stock trading). Incumbents and tech companies were also interviewed to get a comprehensive picture.

Interviews were also conducted with the following authorities: The Bank of England, the Financial Innovation Bureau of the Korean Financial Services Commission, the Luxembourg regulators and Malaysian regulator, the Superintendency of Perú, and the central banks of China, Indonesia, Kenya, Morocco, Rwanda, Sierra Leone, and Uganda.

Finally, the outreach activities also involved meeting with the Korea Fintech Association, the National Payment Corporation of India (NPCI), the Alliance for Financial Inclusion, the NITI Aayog (India) and former officials of the Reserve Bank of India, and the Gates Foundation.

Company Name	Country	Main activity
1debit Inc. ("Chime")	U.S.	Digital Bank
Activehours, Inc. ("Earnin")	U.S.	Domestic Payday P2P Lending
Ant Financial Services Group	China	Online payment services provider
Aye Finance Private Limited	India	Nonbank digital credit provider
Bank Zero	South Africa	Digital bank
Barclays Bank Kenya	Kenya	Bank
Branch International, Inc.	U.S.	Digital credit provider to emerging markets
Cape Innovation and Technology Initiative	South Africa	Tech incubator
CapFloat Financial Services Private Limited	India	Nonbank digital credit provider
CBA Bank	Kenya	Bank
Cellulant	Kenya	Digital payments service provider
Click2Sure Intermediaries Proprietary Limited	South Africa	Digital insurance provider
Data Integrated	Kenya	Digital payments service provider
DIFC Fintech Hive	UAE	Fintech accelerator
First Community Bank	Kenya	Bank
Funding Circle Holdings Plc	U.K.	Digital credit provider to SMEs
Hippo Analytics Inc. ("Hippo Insurance")	U.S.	Digital insurance provider
Honest Fund Co., Ltd	Korea	Marketplace lending platform
Indifi Technologies Pvt. Ltd	India	Digital credit provider to SMEs
Jambopay	Kenya	Digital payments service provider
Jumo World Limited	South Africa	Digital credit provider
Kakao Pay Corp.	Korea	Mobile payment and digital wallet service provider
KB Kookmin Bank	Korea	Bank
KCB Bank	Kenya	Bank
LendingClub Corporation	U.S.	P2P Lending
LendInvest Limited	U.K.	Online mortgage lender and investing platform
Mastarcard	U.S.	Payments service provider
MatchMovePay Pte. Ltd	Singapore	Digital payments provider for enterprises
M-DAQ Pte. Ltd	Singapore	Platform service provider. Allows to prices and trades exchange-traded products in a multitude of currencies
Microsoft Limited	U.K.	Technology and software company
MoneyMatch Sdn Bhd	Malaysia	Cross-border payments company
NISA finance (Pty) Limited	South Africa	Online invoice and purchase order financing platform
Nova Credit Inc.	U.S.	Credit Rating Conversion for U.S. immigrants
OCA (Open Capital Advisors)	Kenya	Financial services and strategy consulting firm
One Mobikwik Systems Private Limited	India	Digital payment services provider
Onfido Limited	U.K.	RegTech
Open Financial Technologies Private Limited	India	Digital bank
PayPal Holdings, Inc.	U.S.	Digital payments and credit provider
PayTabs	Saudi Arabia	Digital payments service provider
Paytm Mobile Solutions Private Limited	**India**	**Payments services provider**
People's Fund Loan Co., Ltd	Korea	Marketplace lending platform
Poynt Co.	U.S.	Digital payments service provider
PrimeKeeper	Malaysia	Digital payments service provider
Razorpay Software Private Limited	India	Digital payments service provider
Samsung Electronics Co., Ltd	Korea	Largest Korean conglomerate, developer of Samsung's fintech payments solution
SC Ventures	Singapore	Innovation, ventures and fintech investments unit of Standard Chartered Bank
Shinhan Bank Co., Ltd	Korea	Bank
Social Finance, Inc.	U.S.	Digital credit provider
Suade Labs Limited	U.K.	RegTech
TALA	Kenya	Digital credit provider
Thisisme	South Africa	Digital identity verification and due diligence platform
Tyme Bank Limited	South Africa	Digital bank
Uala	Argentina	Mobile personal financial management services provider
Uprise.Africa	South Africa	Equity crowdfunding platform
Viva Republica Co., Ltd ("Toss")	Korea	Mobile financial services platform
Wazinsure	Kenya	Digital insurance provider
Woori Bank Developer Lab	Korea	Fintech startup accelerator
Yoco Technologies (Pty) Limited	South Africa	Point-of-sale payments provider for small businesses
Zerodha Commodities Private Limited	India	Online stock trading platform

Annex 2. Measuring Financial Inclusion

We construct a comprehensive financial inclusion index for each of the 52 developing and emerging economies in our sample, composed of both traditional and fintech-driven financial inclusion, spanning across two years—2014 and 2017. A three-stage principal component analysis (PCA) is used to construct the financial inclusion indices. In the first stage, the sub-indices for "access" and "usage" categories in both traditional (FI_T^a, FI_T^u) and fintech-driven component (FI_F^a, FI_F^u) are constructed based on selected variables listed in Annex Table 1, where the weights assigned to each variable are in Annex Figure 1.

A second-stage PCA then combines these access and usage indices—separately for traditional and digital—derived in the first stage, which gives the index for overall traditional and fintech-driven financial inclusion, individually. α and β are the weights assigned to each sub-component, i refers to the country, and $t \epsilon (2014, 2017)$ corresponds to each of the two years.

$$(FI_T)_{it} = \beta_1 (FI_T^a)_{it} + \beta_2 (FI_T^u)_{it} + e_{it}$$

$$(FI_F)_{it} = \alpha_1 (FI_F^a)_{it} + \alpha_2 (FI_F^u)_{it} + \mu_{it}$$

If the model is well specified, $E(e) = 0$ and $E(\mu) = 0$, and the variance of the error term is relatively small compared to the variance of traditional and digital financial inclusion, respectively.

Finally, comprehensive financial inclusion index (FI) is computed by applying PCA on the two indices, traditional financial inclusion index and

Annex Table 1. Selected Variables for Financial Inclusion Indices

Comprehensive Financial Inclusion Index

Traditional Financial Inclusion Index			Digital Financial Inclusion Index		
Access	**Data Source**	**Weight**	**Access**	**Data Source**	**Weight**
Access to bank infrastructure		0.25	**Access to digital infrastructure**		0.125
Number of ATMs per 100,000 adults	IMF FAS		Mobile subscription per 100 people	ITU	
Number of Branches per 100,000 adults	IMF FAS		% of population who have access to internet	ITU	
			Number of registered mobile money agents per 100,000 adults	GSMA; IMF FAS; staff est.	0.25
Usage		0.25	**Usage**		0.125
% of adults with a financial institution account	WB Findex		% of adults who have a mobile account	WB Findex	
% of adults who save at a financial institution	WB Findex		% of adults who use internet to pay	WB Findex	
% of adults with debit cards	WB Findex		% of adults who use mobile phone to receive salary or wages	WB Findex	
% of adults who received wages through a financial institution account	WB Findex		% of adults who use mobile phone to make utility payments	WB Findex	
% of adults who use a financial institution account for utility	WB Findex				

Source: IMF staff calculations.

Note: "Weight" is the weight of the variable in comprehensive index of financial inclusion. IMF FAS = IMF Financial Access Survey; ITU = International Telecommunication Union; WB Findex = World Bank Global Findex Database.

Annex Figure 1. First Stage Principal Components Analysis: Weights

1. Traditional FI Index: Access and Usage Variables (2014, 2017)

2. Fintech-Driven FI Index: Access and Usage Variables (2014, 2017)

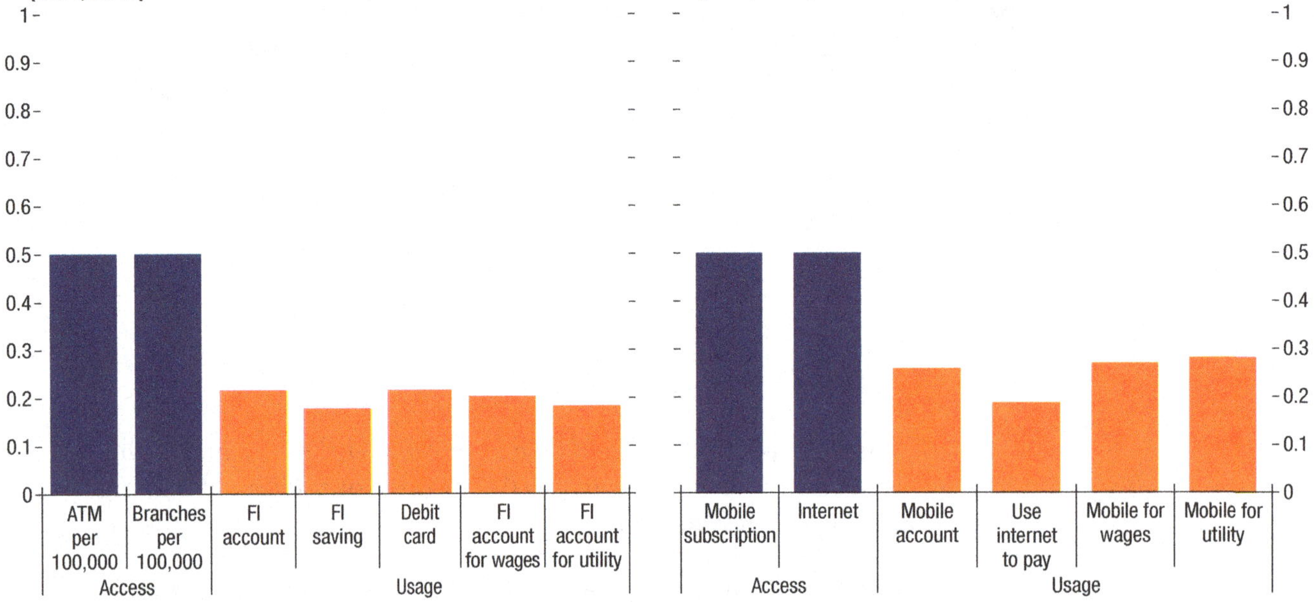

Source: IMF staff calculations.

Note: FI = financial inclusion.

fintech-driven financial inclusion index, in the last stage, where ω is the weight assigned to each of the two subcomponents.[1]

$$FI_{it} = \omega_1 (FI_T)_{it} + \omega_2 (FI_F)_{it} + \omega_{it}$$

To avoid extreme values in variables driving the highest and lowest scores, each variable is winsorized before applying PCA, with cutoff levels at 2nd and 98th percentile. All indices are normalized between 0 and 1 across all countries and years, in which the value of 1 indicates the country in that year has the highest level of financial inclusion among countries and across all years.

Annex Table 2 shows the Loadings in the first component. Annex Table 3 shows, in a cumulative way and by type and dimension of financial inclusion, the amount of the total variance explained by the different components. See Khera and others (2020) for further details.

Annex Table 2. Principal Component Analysis: Loadings

Access (Traditional)	PC_1
ATM per 100,000 population	0.7071
bank per 100,000 population	0.7071
Usage (Traditional)	PC_1
Account at an F.I (%)	0.4842
Saving at an F.I (%)	0.3954
Debit Card (%)	0.4820
F.I account for wages (%)	0.4551
F.I account for utility (%)	0.4120
Access (Fintech-driven)	PC_1
Electricity (%)	0.7071
Internet (%)	0.7071
Usage (Fintech-driven)	PC_1
Mobile account (%)	0.5130
Use internet to pay (%)	0.3722
Mobile for wages (%)	0.5356
Mobile for utility (%)	0.5580

Source: IMF staff calculations.

[1]The purpose of dividing the overall set of financial inclusion into various sub-indices is the following: 1) the various sub-indices provide disaggregated information on financial inclusion, which is useful for policy analysis, and 2) since the sub-indices contain highly inter-correlated indicators, we estimate the sub-indices first, rather than estimating the overall index in one stage with all the indicators at the same time. This is a preferred strategy because PCA is biased toward the weights of indicators, which are highly correlated with each other. Applying the three-stage PCA helps minimize this problem.

Annex Table 3. Cumulative Variance Explained by Principal Components

Access (Traditional)		Access (Fintech-driven)	
PC_1	0.7982	PC_1	0.7884
PC_2	1.0000	PC_2	1.000
Usage (Traditional)		**Usage (Fintech-driven)**	
PC_1	0.7759	PC_1	0.7495
PC_2	0.8986	PC_2	0.9311
PC_3	0.9623	PC_3	0.9774
PC_4	0.9849	PC_4	1.0000
PC_5	1.0000		
		Access and Usage (Fintech-driven)[1]	
		PC_1	0.5435
		PC_2	1.0000
Traditional Financial Inclusion Index		**Fintech-driven Financial Inclusion Index**	
PC_1	0.8448	PC_1	0.5000
PC_2	1.0000	PC_2	1.0000
Overall Financial Inclusion Index			
PC_1	0.6083		
PC_2	1.0000		

Source: IMF staff calculations.

[1]Note that for the fintech-driven financial inclusion index, mobile money agents could not be combined with the other fintech access indicators in the first stage PCA. Doing so would assign a negative weight to mobile money agents as it is negatively correlated with access to the internet and to mobile subscription. Hence, mobile money agents are added at the second stage, as an additional step, for the construction of fintech-driven index.

Annex 3. Determinants of Fintech Lending

Question: We explore drivers of digital lending across countries, focusing on marketplace lending.[1] We ask the following questions: What is the role of basic infrastructure—technology, information, legal—in the development of marketplace lending? Does digital credit[2] develop in countries with more developed financial sector or does fintech lending complement lack of access to finance? Does marketplace lending overcome geographical barriers in access to credit? Do features of banking sector matter for marketplace lending?

Hypotheses:

- **Economic development:** Higher income per capita is expected to increase demand for credit in general, including demand for marketplace lending. Similarly, from a supply-side perspective, investment demand arising from higher income per capita could drive the development of new forms of lending.
- **Internet:** marketplace lending is positively related to the share of population using internet. As the operating platform of marketplace lending is internet, more established internet services would be expected to enable greater marketplace lending activity.
- **Information:** marketplace lending is positively related to easier and wider access to credit information through credit registries. Information (partic-

[1]Marketplace lending involves source of financing that are at least partially open to the public, therefore also including platforms that contribute their own funds in addition to public investors. Our study does not include Big Tech lending (such as credit by e-commerce platforms), digital lending by banks and by mobile platforms as none of these models are open to public.

[2]In this section, we refer to marketplace lending as fintech credit, and marketplace lending to consumers as fintech consumer credit, and marketplace lending to businesses as fintech business credit.

ularly hard information) plays a key role in credit assessment and fintech lending (Bazarbash 2019).

- **Legal infrastructure:** marketplace lending is positively related to the strength of legal rights. A stronger legal infrastructure is key in enforcing the loan contract and dealing with insolvency, which in turn enables credit.
- **Financial development (depth):** marketplace lending is negatively related to the depth of credit provided by traditional lenders (banks). Because it opens access to credit to the underserved population and businesses, digital lending is expected to flourish particularly where traditional lending is underdeveloped.
- **Financial development (access):** lending is typically positively related to financial access. However, the measure of access available to cover all the countries of our sample relates to banks and ATMs, and doesn't include digital access; this should weaken the relation between lending and access.
- **Financial development (efficiency):** marketplace lending is ambiguously related to the efficiency of the banking system (covered by the index). Lower financial efficiency—reflected by elevated spreads and hence more expensive borrowing—could increase demand for alternative financing (negative relationship). However, if elevated spreads reflect a worsening in the credit risk of borrowers, then the relationship would be positive.
- **Geographical barriers:** marketplace lending is negatively related to the geographical presence of bank branches. As lending takes place in a branchless way, digital lending can expand where there are geographical barriers to entry by banks.
- **Features of the Banking Sector (structure, profitability, asset quality):** marketplace lending is ambiguously related to features of banking sector. More concentrated banking could indicate market imperfections and lead to more marketplace lending. By contrast, it could mean digital lenders are subject to growth and entry barriers. Profitability and asset quality are subsets of the financial efficiency index and depending on whether the reason for their change is banking sector-specific or general could have different impacts on marketplace lending.

Country sample and years: We use a panel of 105 countries during 2015–17.

Data source: Data for marketplace lending are provided by the Cambridge Centre for Alternative Finance (CCAF). It is the most comprehensive global data set on alternative finance.

Regression approach: We build a fixed-effect panel regression model with country and year fixed effects. The baseline specification is:

Annex Table 4. Drivers of Total Fintech Credit

Panel regression with country and time fixed effects. The dependent variable is the logarithm of fintech credit to GDP. Sample: 2015–17.

	(1)	(2)	(3)	(4)	(5)	(6)	(7)
Log (PPP GDP per capita)	7.113**	8.007**	8.054**	9.026***	8.908***	13.46**	6.119**
Internet users (% of population)		3.541***	3.539***	3.786***	3.881***	5.299***	4.099***
Depth of Credit Information			0.251	0.247	0.173	−1.086	0.466***
Strength of Legal Rights			0.298	0.329	0.322	4.742***	0.762
Financial Development of Institutions–Depth				−3.363***	−3.528***	−4.893***	−3.379***
Financial Development of Institutions–Access				0.326	0.584	2.628	1.124
Financial Development of Institutions–Efficiency				−0.0237	−0.0379		
Number of Bank Branches (per 1000 km^2)					−0.692		
Bank Concentration (top 5 banks)						−0.295	
Return on Assets of Banks							0.0444
Non-Performing Loans of Banks							−0.784*
Constant	−2.569***	−3.782***	−3.744***	−3.414***	−4.434***	−10.07***	−4.175***
Observations	210	209	206	205	189	102	180
R-squared	0.463	0.542	0.546	0.580	0.630	0.589	0.634
Number of Countries	105	104	103	102	92	58	83

Source: IMF staff calculations.

Note: All explanatory variables are standardized. We use the standard Newey West standard errors and do not cluster the standard errors by country or time in the baseline. As a robustness check, we tried clustering by country, and the results remained almost identical to the baseline. R-squared includes the time and country fixed effects. Robust standard errors in parentheses. *** $p < 0.01$, ** $p < 0.05$, * $p < 0.1$.

$$Y_{it} = \beta_i + \gamma_t + \boldsymbol{\beta} \boldsymbol{X}_{it} + \varepsilon_{it} \qquad (1)$$

where

- Y_{it} is the logarithm of the size of marketplace lending in a country as a share of the country *i*'s nominal GDP at year *t*. Separate regressions are run for total, business, and consumer fintech credit.
- β_i is the country fixed effect accounting for any country-specific level differences.
- γ_t is the time fixed-effect to control for international factors that affect all countries.
- $\boldsymbol{X}_{it}$ collects fintech credit drivers: PPP GDP per capita, internet users, depth of credit information, strength of legal rights, three sub-indices for financial development (depth, access, and efficiency), bank branches per 1,000 square kilometers and features of banking sector (concentration, return on assets, and share of nonperforming loans relative to gross loans).

Results: Annex Table 4 displays the results of panel regression estimates for total fintech lending. For more detailed results, refer to Bazarbash and Beaton (2020).

Annex 4. Digital Financial Inclusion and Growth

Question/motivation: Does greater fintech-driven (digital) financial inclusion in payments translate into higher economic growth? We know that traditional financial inclusion in payments increases economic growth (Sahay and others 2015a). We are interested in exploring whether this relationship also holds for fintech-driven financial inclusion, and if and how does its economic impact differ from traditional financial inclusion.

Methodology: We use a cross-country ordinary least square (OLS) estimation, relating our indices of financial inclusion—traditional and digital indices—at one point in time to subsequent growth over the periods 2011–18 and 2014–18. The baseline estimation equation is as follows:

$$\dot{y}(i)_{2011-18} = \beta_0 + \beta_1 FI(i)_{T,2011} + \beta_2 FI(i)_{F,2011} + \beta_3 X(i)_{2011} + \varepsilon(i)$$

where $\dot{y}$ is real GDP growth, i corresponds to the 52 developing and emerging economies in our sample, and ε is the error term. To address the issue of potential reverse causality, we relate "initial" financial inclusion index—for both traditional ($FI(i)_T$) and fintech-driven ($FI(i)_F$) indices—to growth in the subsequent periods.[1] The vector of control variables ($X(i)$), corresponding to the initial period, includes:

- Level of economic development: log of GDP per capita (source: IMF *World Economic Outlook*)
- Government consumption as a percentage share of GDP (source: World Bank)

[1]For the growth regression over the period 2011–18, we assume that the level of fintech-driven (digital) financial inclusion in 2011 to be the same as 2014, due to data limitations.

- Foreign direct investment (FDI) as a percentage share of GDP (source: IMF *World Economic Outlook*)
- Inflation: annual percentage change in consumer prices (source: IMF *World Economic Outlook*)
- Level of financial depth: log of private credit as a percentage share of GDP (source: World Bank Development Indicators)
- Dummy variables for regional grouping: Asia, Middle East and Central Asia, Latin America, emerging Europe, sub-Saharan Africa

Robustness checks and additional analysis: We conducted a range of robustness checks and some additional analysis, including:

- Estimating the contribution of fintech credit: to analyze if fintech credit has an impact on growth, we add the logarithm of the total new originations of fintech credit as a share of nominal GDP in 2015 as an additional explanatory variable to the regression covering the period 2014–18. Estimates indicate that the effect of fintech credit on growth is not statistically significant, while the impact of other variables remain the same as the baseline estimates.
- Removing the cyclical effects in GDP: we replace the dependent variable with the average of the detrended real GDP growth, by using Hodrick-Prescott (HP) filter to obtain the stationary series.
- Estimating the contribution of comprehensive financial inclusion: we replace the fintech-driven financial inclusion index and traditional financial inclusion index with the initial level of comprehensive financial inclusion. Initial levels of comprehensive financial inclusion are found to have a positive impact on per capita GDP growth, but this impact is not statistically significant once an indicator of traditional financial sector depth (domestic private credit-to-GDP ratio) is added to the regressions.
- Using the Financial Development Index (FDI) instead of private credit (% of GDP). The FDI is based on the database of Sahay and others (2015), updated at http://data.imf.org/fdindex.
- Using the three-year averages (over 2009–11 and 2011–14) for government consumption, FDI, and private credit (%GDP) instead of the initial period only.

In all cases, the results were similar to the baseline estimates. For a more detailed discussion, refer to Khera and others (2020).

Annex Table 5. Results: Growth and Digital Financial Inclusion

	(1)	(2)	(3)	(4)	(5)	(6)	(7)	(8)	(9)	(10)	(11)	(12)
	OLS estimation: Real GDP growth rate (2011–18)						OLS estimation: Real GDP growth rate (2014–18)					
Log (GDP per capita)	−0.0879***	−0.0940***	−0.0880***	−0.0933***	−0.0837***	−0.0793***	−0.0465***	−0.0439***	−0.0447***	−0.0474***	−0.0473***	−0.0419***
Inflation	−0.0035	−0.0085**	−0.0091**	−0.0075*	−0.0080*	−0.0099**	−0.0015	−0.0039	−0.0036	−0.0029	−0.0030	−0.0018
Traditional F.I Index	0.157	0.241**	0.176	0.129	0.004	−0.144	0.0606	0.109	0.112	0.024	0.023	−0.105
Digital F.I Index	0.272*	0.364***	0.376***	0.311**	0.314**	0.371***	0.175**	0.150**	0.148**	0.129*	0.130*	0.188**
Gov. Consumption (% of GDP)		−0.016***	−0.016***	−0.016***	−0.016***	−0.012***		−0.0096***	−0.0096***	−0.0091***	−0.0091***	−0.0048*
FDI (% of GDP)			−0.0025		−0.0038*	−0.0046**			0.0007		−0.0002	−0.0001
Log (private credit) (% of GDP)				0.0401**	0.0504**	0.0488*				0.0357**	0.0359**	0.0347*
Constant	0.929***	1.182***	1.141***	1.064***	0.970***	0.950***	0.468***	0.578***	0.584***	0.502***	0.500***	0.470***
Regional dummy	No	No	No	No	No	Yes	No	No	No	No	No	Yes
N	48	48	48	47	47	47	50	50	50	49	49	49
adj. R^2	0.238	0.442	0.451	0.476	0.509	0.543	0.154	0.370	0.356	0.432	0.418	0.486

Source: IMF staff calculations.

Note: Robust standard errors are in parentheses. *** $p < 0.01$, ** $p < 0.05$, * $p < 0.1$.

Annex 5. Determinants of Digital Financial Inclusion

Question/motivation: What drives the adoption of fintech-driven financial inclusion in payments? Why do some countries have higher adoption rates than others? What is the relationship between the adoption of fintech-driven payments and the level of traditional financial inclusion in a country? In other words, is fintech-driven financial inclusion complementing or substituting traditional means of financial inclusion?

Methodology: When looking at the drivers of fintech-driven financial inclusion, two aspect matter—the drivers of access (i.e. supply) and the drivers of usage (i.e. demand)—which we estimate using two separate regressions. The estimation procedure relies on two alternative approaches:

- *Ordinary least squares (OLS) regression*: the drivers of access to fintech is estimated using an OLS regression, where mobile money agents (per 100,000 adults) is the dependent variable.
- *Fractional logit regression*: the drivers of fintech's usage is estimated through a fractional logit regression (Papke and Wooldridge 1996), using our newly-computed fintech usage index (Annex 2). The fractional logit regression accounts for the fractional nature of the dependent variable (the financial usage index falls in the unit interval [0,1]), and handles the extreme values of 0 and 1 without having to manipulate the data.

The equations are estimated separately for 2014 and 2017, as well as jointly (pooled estimation). The results in the table below refer to the pooled regression. The sample consists of 52 low-income and developing economies for which we compute the financial inclusion index (Annex 2).

To account for the fact that access and usage of financial services go hand-in-hand, we use the digital usage index as one of the determinants for access to fintech services, and vice-versa. To avoid problems with endogeneity, we use the lagged values of the fintech usage index to explain its impact on fintech access (and vice versa). We draw from the existing literature for the selection of the other main determinants of financial inclusion:

- Level of economic development: log of GDP per capita (source: IMF *World Economic Outlook*)
- Financial sector efficiency: overhead costs to assets used as a proxy (source: World Bank Finstat)
- Level of competition in the financial sector: bank concentration defined as assets of three largest commercial banks as a share of total commercial banking assets used as a proxy (source: World Bank Finstat)
- Financial stability: log of NPL as a share of total gross loans used as a proxy (source: IMF Financial Soundness Indicators)
- Governance/institutional quality: rule of law, scaled from 0 to 1 with 1 signifying strongest rule of law, as an indicator of the perception of confidence in the rules of the society used as a proxy (data source: World Justice Project)
- Urban population: urban population as a share of total population (data source: World Bank Development Indicator)

To avoid reverse causality, we used one-period lagged values for the explanatory variables.

Annex Table 6. Determinants of Fintech Usage

	(1)	(2)	(3)	(4)	(5)	(6)	(7)	(8)	(9)	(10)	(11)	(12)	(13)	(14)
	Fractional Logit Estimation: Fintech Usage Financial inclusion index (*t*)													
Trad. Access F.I Index ($t-3$)	−3.658***	−2.418**	−4.266***	−4.181***	−4.205***	−4.006***	−4.008***	−3.909***	−2.030*	−1.912*	−1.980*	−1.996*	−2.300**	−2.228**
Trad. Usage F.I Index ($t-3$)	4.692***	4.449***	5.092***	5.388***	5.654***	5.660***	5.346***	5.354***	4.956***	5.199***	5.311***	5.322***	4.935***	4.882***
Fintech. Access F.I Index ($t-3$)		0.211	1.236	1.165	1.425*	1.814**	0.374	0.607	1.354*	1.534**	1.669**	1.658**	−0.272	−0.229
Mobile Money Agents ($t-1$)		0.00302***	0.00201***	0.00170***	0.00184***	0.00169***	0.00114*	0.00107*	0.00264***	0.00235***	0.00248***	0.00249***	0.00170**	0.00166**
Log (NPL) ($t-1$)			0.501**	0.470**	0.511**	0.481**	0.330	0.320						
Log (GDP Per capita)									−0.538**	−0.578**	−0.563**	−0.571**	−0.135	−0.0975
Overhead cost To assets ($t-1$)				0.0979	0.0923	0.122*	0.112	0.127*		0.0898	0.0808	0.0794	0.102	0.108*
Rule of law ($t-1$)					−0.0122	−0.0135	0.000135	−0.000901			−0.00716	−0.00710	0.00307	0.00284
Urban Population ($t-1$)						−0.00780		−0.00410				0.000578		−0.00276
Year fixed effect	No	No	No	No	No	No	Yes	Yes	No	No	No	No	Yes	Yes
N	96	96	80	79	79	79	79	79	95	95	95	95	95	95

Source: IMF staff calculations.

Note: Robust standard errors are in parentheses. *** $p < 0.01$, ** $p < 0.05$, * $p < 0.1$.

Annex Table 7. Determinants of Fintech Access

	(1)	(2)	(3)	(4)	(5)	(6)	(7)	(8)	(9)	(10)	(11)	(12)	(13)	(14)	(15)
	OLS Estimation: Mobile money agents per 100,000 adults (*t*)														
Trad. Access F.I. Index ($t-3$)	−539.2***	−374.0*	−358.9*	−346.9*	−207.7	−226.1	−203.0	−224.2	−72.56	−48.74	46.53	104.9	104.8	99.74	99.08
Trad. Usage F.I. Index ($t-3$)	119.8	22.13	82.98	93.75	166.4	52.00	85.29	−61.68	105.4	156.5	166.7	73.45	72.18	−24.69	−33.33
Fintech. Usage F.I. Index ($t-3$)		396.4**	307.5	225.7	131.1	102.7	179.9	153.0	408.9**	321.3	250.9	189.2	185.5	244.8	227.4
Log (NPL) ($t-1$)		94.18***	83.67***	70.26**	51.97	39.97	40.78	24.98							
Log (GDP per capita) ($t-1$)									−109.0***	−102.2***	−113.9***	−146.8***	−143.9***	−131.2***	−116.0**
Overhead cost to assets ($t-1$)			28.82**	43.95***	51.91***	54.16***	51.94***	54.60***		24.95**	33.15***	41.67***	41.90***	41.87***	43.03***
Bank concentration ($t-1$)				−3.817**	−3.273**	−3.149**	−3.667**	−3.576**			−3.151**	−3.183***	−3.133**	−3.193***	−2.938**
Urban population ($t-1$)					−2.665*	−3.013**	−2.462*	−2.846**				6.235***	6.233***	6.275***	6.265***
Rule of law ($t-1$)						3.826*		4.531**					3.826*		4.531**
Year fixed effect	No	No	No	No	No	No	Yes	Yes	No	No	No	No	No	Yes	Yes
N	96	96	80	79	79	79	79	79	96	95	94	94	94	94	94
Adj. R^2	0.102	0.256	0.303	0.354	0.376	0.397	0.408	0.441	0.242	0.278	0.318	0.390	0.383	0.433	0.428

Source: IMF staff calculations.

Note: Robust standard errors are in parentheses. *** $p < 0.01$, ** $p < 0.05$, * $p < 0.1$.

References

Adrian, Tobias, and Tommaso Mancini-Griffoli. 2019. "The Rise of Digital Money." IMF Fintech Note No. 19/01, International Monetary Fund, Washington, DC.

Agur, Itai, Soledad Martinez Peria, and Celine Rochon, 2020. "Digital Financial Services and the Pandemic: Opportunities and Risks for Emerging and Developing Economies." Special Series on COVID-19. International Monetary Fund, Washington, DC (forthcoming).

Alliance for Financial Inclusion (AFI). 2017. "Denarau Action Plan: The AFI Network Commitment to Gender and Women's Financial Inclusion." Kuala Lumpur. https://www.afi-global.org/publications/2377/Denarau-Action-Plan-The-AFI-Network-Commitment-to-Gender-and-Women-s-Financial-Inclusion.

Alliance for Financial Inclusion (AFI). 2018. "Fintech for Financial Inclusion: A Framework for Digital Financial Transformation." Kuala Lumpur. https://www.afi-global.org/publications/2844/FinTech-for-Financial-Inclusion-A-Framework-for-Digital-Financial-Transformation.

Amidžić, Goran, Alexander Massara, and Andre Mialou. 2014. "Assessing Countries' Financial Inclusion Standing – A New Composite Index." IMF Working Paper No. 14/36, International Monetary Fund, Washington, DC.

Ayyagari, Meghana, Asli Demirgüç-Kunt, and Vojislav Maksimovic. 2017. "SME Finance." World Bank Policy Research Working Paper No. 8241, World Bank, Washington, DC.

Bazarbash, Majid. 2019. "FinTech in Financial Inclusion: Machine Learning Applications in Assessing Credit Risk." IMF Working Paper No. 19/109, International Monetary Fund, Washington, DC.

Bazarbash, Majid, and Kimberly Beaton. 2020. “Filling the Gap: Digital Credit and Financial Inclusion.” IMF Working Paper, International Monetary Fund, Washington, DC. (forthcoming)

Beck, Thorsten, Asli Demirgüç-Kunt, and Maria Soledad Martinez Peria. 2007. “Reaching Out: Access to and Use of Banking Service across Countries.” *Journal of Financial Economics* 85: 234–66.

Berkmen, Pelin, Kimberly Beaton, Dmitry Gershenson, Javier Arze del Granado, Kotaro Ishi, Marie Kim, Emanuel Kopp, and Marina Rousset. 2019. “Fintech in Latin America and the Caribbean: Stocktaking.” IMF Working Paper 19/71, International Monetary Fund, Washington, DC.

Blancher, Nicolas, Max Appendino, Aidyn Bibolov, Armand Fouejieu, Jiawei Li, Anta Ndoye, Alexandra Panagiotakopoulou, Wei Shi, and Tetyana Sydorenko. 2019. “Financial Inclusion of Small and Medium-Sized Enterprises in the Middle East and Central Asia.” IMF Departmental Paper No. 19/02, International Monetary Fund, Washington, DC.

Brunnermeier, Markus, James Harold, and Jean-Pierre Landau. 2019. “The Digitalization of Money.” NBER Working Paper No. 26300, National Bureau of Economic Research, Cambridge, MA.

Camara, Noelia, and David Tuesta. 2017. “Measuring Financial Inclusion: A Multidimensional Index.” Bank of Morocco – CEMLA – IFC Satellite Seminar at the ISI World Statistics Congress on Financial Inclusion, Marrakech, July 14.

Carrière-Swallow, Yan, and Vikram Haksar. 2019. “The Economics and Implications of Data: An Integrated Perspective.” IMF Departmental Paper No. 19/16, International Monetary Fund, Washington, DC.

Carstens, Agustín. 2018. “Big Tech in Finance and New Challenges for Public Policy.” Keynote address to the FT Banking Summit, London, December 4. https://www.bis.org/speeches/sp181205.htm

Čihák, Martin, and Ratna Sahay. 2020. “Finance and Inequality.” IMF Staff Discussion Note No. 20/02, International Monetary Fund, Washington, DC.

Citi. 2020. “Banking the Next Billion: Digital Financial Inclusion in Action.”

Claessens, Stijin, Jon Frost, Grant Turner, and Feng Zhu. 2018. “Fintech Credit Markets Around the World: Size, Drivers and Policy Issues.” *BIS Quarterly Review* (September): 29–49.

Dabla-Norris, Era, Yixi Deng, Anna Ivanova, Izabela Karpowicz, Filiz Unsal, Eva VanLeemput, and Joyce Wong. 2015a. “Financial Inclusion: Zooming in on Latin America.” IMF Working Paper No. 15/206, International Monetary Fund, Washington, DC.

Dabla-Norris, Era, Yan Ji, Robert Townsend, and D. Filiz Unsal. 2015b. "Distinguishing Constraints on Financial Inclusion and Their Impact on GDP, TFP, and Inequality." NBER Working Paper No. 20821, National Bureau of Economic Research, Cambridge, MA.

Deléchat, Corinne, Monique Newiak, Rui Xu, Fan Yang, and Goksu Aslan. 2018. "What is Driving Women's Financial Inclusion Across Countries?" IMF Working Paper No. 18/38, International Monetary Fund, Washington, DC.

Demirgüç-Kunt, Asli, and Leora Klapper. 2012. "Measuring Financial Inclusion: The Global Findex Database." World Bank Policy Research Working Paper No. 6025, World Bank, Washington, DC.

Demirgüç-Kunt, Asli, Leora Klapper, Dorothe Singer, Saniya Ansar, and Jake Hess. 2018. "The Global Findex Database: Measuring Financial Inclusion and the Fintech Revolution." World Bank Group, Washington, DC.

De Roure, Calebe, Loriana Pelizzon, and Anjar V. Thakor. 2018. "P2P Lenders Versus Banks: Creak Skimming or Bottom Fishing?" SAFE Working Paper No. 206, Goethe University, Sustainable Architecture for Finance in Europe, Frankfurt.

Faux, Zeke. 2020. "From Micro-Credit to Major Debt." *Bloomberg Business Week*, February 17.

Financial Conduct Authority, 2018. "Cyber and Technology Resilience: Themes from Cross-Sector Survey 2017–18." November.

Financial Stability Board (FSB). 2017. "Financial Stability Implications from FinTech: Supervisory and Regulatory Issues that Merit Authorities' Attention." Basel. https://www.fsb.org/wp-content/uploads/R270617.pdf

Financial Stability Board (FSB). 2019. "FinTech and Market Structure in Financial Services: Market Developments and Potential Financial Stability Implications." Basel. https://www.fsb.org/wp-content/uploads/P140219.pdf

FinRegLab. "The Use of Cash-Flow Data in Underwriting Credit." 2019. https://finreglab.org/wp-content/uploads/2019/07/FRL_Research-Report_Final.pdf

Fu, Jonathan, and Mrinal Mishra. 2020. "The Global Impact of COVID-19 on Fintech Adoption." Swiss Finance Institute Research Paper, No. 20–38, Zürich.

Fung, B. S. C., Kim P. Huynh, and Leonard Sabetti. 2014. "The Impact of Retail Payment Innovations on Cash Usage." *Journal of Financial Market Infrastructure* 3 (1): 3–31.

Fuster, Andreas, Matthew Plosser, Philipp Schnabl, and James Vickery. 2018. "The Role of Technology in Mortgage Lending." NBER Working Paper No. 24500, National Bureau of Economic Research, Cambridge, MA.

Group of Seven (G7). 2019. "Investigating the Impact of Global Stablecoins." G7 Working Group on Stablecoins, October. https://www.bis.org/cpmi/publ/d187.pdf

Group of Twenty (G20). 2016. "G20 High-Level Principles for Digital Financial Inclusion." http://www.g20.utoronto.ca/2016/high-level-principles-for-digital-financial-inclusion.pdf

Group of Twenty (G20). 2019. "G20 Fukuoka Policy Priorities on Aging and Financial Inclusion." https://www.gpfi.org/sites/gpfi/files/documents/G20%20Fukuoka%20Policy%20Priorities%20on%20Aging%20and%20Financial%20Inclusion.pdf

GSMA. 2016. "Driving a Price Revolution: Mobile Money in International Remittances." https://www.gsma.com/mobilefordevelopment/wp-content/uploads/2016/10/2016_GSMA_Driving-a-price-revolution-Mobile-money-in-international-remittances.pdf

GSMA. 2018. "The Future of Mobile Money Agent Distribution Networks" Distribution 2.0. https://www.gsma.com/mobilefordevelopment/wp-content/uploads/2018/07/Distribution-2.0-The-future-of-mobile-money-agent-distribution-networks-1.pdf

Gutierrez, Eva, and Sandeep Singh. 2013. "What Regulatory Frameworks Are More Conducive to Mobile Banking? Empirical Evidence from Findex Data." World Bank Policy Research Working Paper No. 6652, Washington, DC.

Hau, Harald, Yi Huang, Hongzhe Shan, and Zixia Sheng. 2018. "TechFin in China: Credit Market Completion and its Growth Effect." Presented at EC 2342 China Economy Seminar, Harvard University, Cambridge, MA, March 2.

Honohan, Patrick. 2008. "Cross-Country Variation in Household Access to Financial Services." *Journal of Banking and Finance* 32: 2493–500.

International Monetary Fund (IMF). 2018a. "The Bali Fintech Agenda." IMF Policy Paper, Washington, DC.

International Monetary Fund. 2018b. "Kenya's Success in Boosting Financial Inclusion." IMF Country Report No. 18/296, Washington, DC.

International Monetary Fund. 2019a. "Fintech—The Experience So Far." Policy Paper No. 19/024, Washington, DC.

International Monetary Fund. 2019b. "Review of the Funds' Strategy on Anti-Money Laundering and Combating the Financing of Terrorism." IMF Policy Paper, International Monetary Fund, Washington, DC.

International Monetary Fund. 2020. "Reaching Households in Emerging and Developing Economies: Citizen ID, Socioeconomic Data, and Digital Delivery." Special Series on Fiscal Policies to Respond to COVID-19, Washington, DC.

International Monetary Fund. 2020a. "Digitization in Sub-Saharan Africa." *Regional Economic Outlook: Sub-Saharan Africa*, Washington, DC.

Islam, Asif, Silvia Muzi, and Jorge Luis Rodriguez Meza. 2018. "Does Mobile Money Use Increase Firms' Investment? Evidence from Enterprise Surveys in Kenya, Uganda, and Tanzania." *Small Business Economics* (51): 687–708.

Jack, William, and Tavneet Suri. 2011 "Mobile Money: The Economics of M-Pesa." NBER Working Paper No. 16721, National Bureau of Economic Research, Cambridge, MA.

Jack, William, and Tavneet Suri. 2014. "Risk Sharing and Transactions Costs: Evidence from Kenya's Mobile Money Revolution." *American Economic Review* 104 (1): 183–223.

Jack, William, and Tavneet Suri. 2016. "The Long-Run Poverty and Gender Impacts of Mobile Money." *Science* 354 (6317): 1288–92.

Jagtiani, Julapa, and Catharine Lemieux. 2017. "Fintech Lending: Financial Inclusion, Risk Pricing, and Alternative Information." Federal Reserve Bank of Philadelphia Working Paper No. 17–17, Philadelphia.

Jahan, Sarwat, Jayendu De, Fazurin Jamaludin, Piyaporn Sodsriwiboon, and Cormac Sullivan. 2019. "The Financial Inclusion Landscape in the Asia-Pacific Region: A Dozen Key Findings." IMF Working Paper No. 19/79, International Monetary Fund, Washington, DC.

Kaffenberger, Michelle, Edoardo Totolo, and Matthew Soursourian. 2018. "A Digital Credit Revolution: Insights from Borrowers in Kenya and Tanzania." CGAP-FSD Working Paper, October, Consultative Group to Assist the Poor, Washington, DC.

Khera, Purva, Stephanie Ng, Sumiko Ogawa, and Ratna Sahay. 2020. "Can FinTech Unlock Financial Inclusion in Emerging and Developing Economies?" IMF Working Paper, International Monetary Fund, Washington, DC. (forthcoming)

Khera, Purva, Sumiko Ogawa, and Ratna Sahay. 2020. "Women and Fintech: Are Gender Gaps Closing (forthcoming)

Lashitew, Addisu A., Rob van Tulder, and Yann Liasse. 2019. "Mobile Phones for Financial Inclusion: What Explains the Diffusion of Mobile Money Innovations?" *Research Policy* 48 (5): 1201–15.

Loukoianova, Elena, and Yongzheng Yang. 2018. "Financial Inclusion in Asia-Pacific." IMF Asia and Pacific Departmental Paper No. 18/17, International Monetary Fund, Washington, DC.

Loukoianova, Elena, Sonja Davidovic, Cormac Sullivan, and Hervé Tourpe. 2019. "Strategy for Fintech Applications in the Pacific Island Countries." IMF APD Departmental Paper No. 19/14, International Monetary Fund, Washington, DC.

Lukonga, Inutu. 2018. "Fintech, Inclusive Growth, and Cyber Risks: Focus on the MENAP and CCA Regions." IMF Working Paper No. 18/201, International Monetary Fund, Washington, DC.

Papke, Leslie E., and Jeffrey M. Wooldridge. 1996. "Econometric Methods for Fractional Response Variables with an Application to 401(k) Plan Participation Rates." *Journal of Applied Econometrics* 11 (6): 619–32.

Patwardhan, Anju, Ken Singleton, and Kai Schmitz. 2018. "Financial Inclusion in the Digital Age." CreditEase, International Finance Corporation, the Stanford Graduate School of Business, Palo Alto, CA.

Rau, Raghavendra P. 2019. "Law, Trust, and the Development of Crowdfunding." Cambridge Judge Business School, Cambridge University, Cambridge, UK.

Rojas-Suárez, Liliana, and Maria Alejandra Amado. 2014. "Understanding Latin America's Financial Inclusion Gap." CGD Working Paper No. 367, Center for Global Development, Washington DC.

Rojas-Suárez, Liliana. 2016. "Financial Inclusion in Latin America: Facts, Obstacles and Central Banks' Policy Issues." IDB Discussion Paper No. DP-464, Inter-American Development Bank, Washington DC.

Sahay, Ratna, Martin Čihák, Papa N'Diaye, Adolfo Barajas, Srobona Mitra, Annette Kyobe, Yen Nian Mooi, and Seyed Reza Yousefi. 2015a. "Financial Inclusion: Can It Meet Multiple Macroeconomic Goals?" IMF Staff Discussion Note No. 15/17, International Monetary Fund, Washington, DC.

Sahay, Ratna, Martin Čihák, Papa N'Diaye, Adolfo Barajas, Ran Bi, Diana Ayala, Yuan Gao, Annette Kyobe, Lam Nguyen, Christian Saborowski, Katsiaryna Svirydzenka, and Seyed Reza Yousefi. 2015b. "Rethinking Financial Deepening: Stability and Growth in Emerging Markets." IMF Staff Discussion Note No. 15/08, International Monetary Fund, Washington, DC.

Sioson, Erica Paula, and Chul Ju Kim. 2019. "Closing the Gender Gap in Financial Inclusion through Fintech." ADB Institute Policy Brief No. 2019–3, Asian Development Bank, Manila.

Staschen, Stefan, and Patrick Meagher. 2018. "Basic Regulatory Enablers for Digital Financial Services." CGAP Focus Note 109, Consultative Group to Assist the Poor, Washington, DC.

Svirydzenka, Katsiaryna. 2016. "Introducing a New Broad-based Index of Financial Development." IMF Working Paper No. 16/5, International Monetary Fund, Washington, DC.

Sy, Amadou N. R., Rodolfo Maino, Alexander Massara, Hector Perez-Saiz, and Preya Sharma. 2019. "Fintech in Sub-Saharan African Countries: A Game Changer?" African Departmental Paper No. 19/04, International Monetary Fund, Washington, DC.

Tarazi, Michael, and Paul Breloff. 2010. "Nonbank E-Money Issuers: Regulatory Approaches to Protecting Customer Funds." CGAP Focus Note No. 56629, Consultative Group to Assist the Poor, Washington, DC.

Taylor, Charles R., Christopher Wilson, Eija Holttinen, and Anastasiia Morozova. 2020. "Institutional Arrangements for Fintech Regulation and Supervision." IMF Fintech Note, International Monetary Fund, Washington, DC.

Transunion. 2019." FinTechs Continue to Drive Personal Loan Growth." https://newsroom.transunion.com/fintechs-continue-to-drive-personal-loans-to-record-levels/

UNSGSA FinTech Working Group and CCAF. 2019. "Early Lessons on Regulatory Innovations to Enable Inclusive FinTech: Innovation Offices, Regulatory Sandboxes, and RegTech." Office of the UNSGSA and CCAF: New York and Cambridge, UK.

Made in the USA
Monee, IL
02 November 2026

67381626R00046